LUFTWAFFE IN COMBAT 1939-45

VOICES FROM THE LUFTWAFFE

BY BOB CARRUTHERS

Pen & Sword
AVIATION

This edition published in 2012 by
Pen & Sword Aviation
An imprint of
Pen & Sword Books Ltd
47 Church Street
Barnsley
South Yorkshire
S70 2AS

First published in Great Britain in 2011 in digital format by
Coda Books Ltd.

Copyright © Coda Books Ltd, 2011
Published under licence by Pen & Sword Books Ltd.

ISBN 978 1 78159 111 6

Printed and bound by CPI Group (UK) Ltd, Croydon, CR0 4YY

Pen & Sword Books Ltd incorporates the Imprints of Pen & Sword Aviation, Pen & Sword Family History, Pen & Sword Maritime, Pen & Sword Military, Pen & Sword Discovery, Pen & Sword Politics, Pen & Sword Atlas, Pen & Sword Archaeology, Wharncliffe Local History, Wharncliffe True Crime, Wharncliffe Transport, Pen & Sword Select, Pen & Sword Military Classics, Leo Cooper, The Praetorian Press, Claymore Press, Remember When, Seaforth Publishing and Frontline Publishing

For a complete list of Pen & Sword titles please contact
PEN & SWORD BOOKS LIMITED
47 Church Street, Barnsley, South Yorkshire, S70 2AS, England
E-mail: enquiries@pen-and-sword.co.uk
Website: www.pen-and-sword.co.uk

CONTENTS

THE PROPAGANDA WAR
FROM THE ENGLISH LANGUAGE VERSION OF DER ADLER

From his office at Rostock-Marienehe Dr. Heinkel watched his works pilots trying out their new machines. A field-glass is always handy, so that he can follow their trial flights.

Karl Born, Luftwaffe pilot. "The Russian air force was very bad. They hurled all sorts of stuff down, stones, bits of iron. It was all very primitive."

Alfred Wagner, Luftwaffe fighter pilot. "I volunteered for the Luftwaffe when I was 17. To me, it was a marvellous adventure. If we were asked to volunteer to fly somewhere, I was always first in the queue!"

The famous Stuka dive bomber has become synonymous with the Wehrmacht of the Blitzkrieg era. The unique gull wing configuration made the sinister shape this dive bomber readily distinguishable. However the cumbersome non-retractable landing gear contributed to the very slow air speed rendered the Stuka highly vulnerable to Allied fighters. This glaring drawback was cruelly demonstrated in the Battle of Britain where the losses were so high that the aircraft had to be withdrawn from frontline service.

INTRODUCTION TO THE
WEHRMACHT INTERVIEWS

For most people alive at the time, the Second World War is a distant, if painful, memory. For very many more, it is just history, something that happened before they were born and made no impact on their lives or their recollections. However, for those who served and survived, the recollections are as vivid as they were at the time they occurred and nearly sixty years on, they remain vivid down to the last fine detail.

Until recently, the picture has been somewhat incomplete. The generals and politicians have written their memoirs, the regimental histories have found their way into print, some of the participants have set down their experiences, the films, the videos, the documentaries have been made. It is, however, the victors who write history, and the Second World War has been no exception. Now, a group German veterans who have kept silent for nearly sixty years have come forward with accounts of their own war.

In their youth, they served the Third Reich and their Führer for the six years the War lasted and came away with impressions and memories of the conflict from the sharpest of sharp ends - the early halcyon days of the blitzkrieg, the hazards and rigours of the Russian campaign, the discomforts of the U-boat war, the war in the air and the last days of Berlin in 1945 as the thousand-year Reich went down in the blood, flames and destruction of total ruin.

The Third Reich had many faces, and the German veterans who tell their stories in this book came to the Second World War from different and sometimes surprising perspectives. For instance, Detlef Radbruch, who fought with the Luftwaffe, had little time for Hitler and actually came from an anti-Nazi family, but as a soldier, he still believes, 'you have to do your duty'. Hanno Rittau, who served in a Luftwaffe anti-aircraft unit, says much the same thing: 'We had to defend out home and we had to defend our country, and that's what we tried to do.'

Heinz Reiners joined the Kriegsmarine because his father had served in the German Navy during the First World War.

'So his son had to do the same in the Second! But it wasn't just that. We were young, we were enthusiastic. The propaganda we heard told us that only the Germans were worth anything, all the others were nothing. That's the way we were brought up in our youth.'

For Karl Born, a volunteer who joined the Luftwaffe, his war service was a natural continuation of his training as a glider pilot, which began when he was only thirteen, in 1936.

'At that time, the first flying groups had been set up in the Hitler Youth. We were supervised by the German Air Sport Association which had been founded after the First World War by former airmen. They had been forced to switch to gliders because Germany wasn't allowed to build planes with engines any more. I took various glider pilot exams in this Hitler Youth Flying group and after that the air pilot license for gliders, which permitted me to fly gliders loaded with up to ten people'.

Karl Born found it all a great adventure, though his sense of adventure was afterwards tempered by his war experiences.

'I volunteered when I was seventeen and when I was twenty, in 1941, I went on my first mission. Flying was enormous fun, and I was full of enthusiasm for it. If we were asked to flying somewhere, anywhere, I always volunteered straight away. Of course, it was a good feeling to survive aerial battles, but in retrospect, later, when you reviewed it all, you had to say that it was all madness. The war, every war, shooting at men you'd never seen before...I must say that today, I wouldn't want to volunteer.'

Wolfgang Reinhardt was another volunteer for whom the War was just an extension of peace-time activity. Reinhardt belonged first to the Jungvolk, afterwards to the Hitler Youth, and that meant that between the ages of six and sixteen, when he volunteered, he was preparing for war and knew little else.

'I was a recruit in the Army NCO school, Potsdam-Reiche, the élite school in Germany. Whoever went through its doors could be proud to have been there, you could walk 3 centimetres taller. All the training was geared to war. We were trained on mortars and machine guns; and made mock attacks on bunkers, although it wasn't all that much of a pretence because live rounds and shells were used. The training was tough. We had to face all the dangers of real battle, and its discomforts, too.

'I'll give you an example. There was a river in eastern Prussia called the Liebe, a small river perhaps one metre deep. We were ordered to about turn, and march into the Liebe about turn and march out of the Liebe, about turn back into the Liebe again, holding rifles and machine guns up so that they didn't get wet. We had to put up with the cold, too. Potsdam in winter was ice cold, lousy cold.

'As a training exercise, we were ordered to attack a town. We had hardly started when the command came to stop. 'Artillery, change of positions, you must dig yourselves in.' And we sat there for hours in that cold in the snow before the word came that we could continue and the change of positions was over.

A squadron of He-111 bombers

'It went to extremes. We had to run around the training areas with full pack and equipment, not walking, but running over three or four kilometres of the training areas, including the field packs we had. Later the field pack was replaced by a storm pack. We had to climb over walls, over barbed wire, through a pipe, over the wall again, and that went on for an hour or more'.

Eckhart Strasosky was a leader in the Hitler Youth before he joined the Wehrmacht on 1 December 1939 and later fought in Yugoslavia and Russia. At eighteen, Strasosky had already commanded a group of young fourteen- to eighteen- year olds and was predestined for the officer corps from the start.

'I was an officer at twenty-two. At that time, once the war had begun, every boy of the right age volunteered to join the Wehrmacht. I was one of them. But I didn't really understand anything about politics and there were many others like me. Before the war when we were ten or fourteen years old, we didn't even realise that we were being prepared for war, through military fitness training or sporting achievements. We weren't told what the end of it all was going to be.'

Hajo Hermann, later to become a famous Luftwaffe ace, approached the War from a predominantly political point of view. The Treaty of Versailles of 1919, which ended the First World War, had reorganised areas of Europe in such a way that German minorities found themselves severed from Germany and placed under the rule of two new countries: Czechoslovakia and Poland. In both countries, or so Adolf Hitler claimed, they were suffering discrimination.

Millions of resentful Germans, including Hajo Hermann, believed him. They were mollified when the problem of the German 'exiles' in the Sudetenland of Czechoslovakia was solved at Munich in 1938: the agreement made there by Britain, France, Germany and Italy transferred the Sudeten districts to the Third Reich. In 1939, however, the Germans in Poland had yet to be rescued. When Germany precipitated the Second World War by attacking Poland on 1 September 1939, Hajo Hermann was firmly convinced that it had been a great wrong to consign a predominantly German population to the Poles.

'That had to be redressed. Hitler's suggestion, to hold a referendum was refused by the Poles, who were unfortunately supported in their decision by the British and Americans. And that led to the conflict. At any rate, I participated in that war and I always said to myself that we did what we just had to do, what Germans had to do. If we had accepted the injustice, then we would have been the worst idiots ever.

'I was a bit older than most, twenty-five or twenty-six when the War began in 1939, and I'd studied history, listened to my teachers talking about the First World War, the Treaty of Versailles and that shameful Paragraph 231 which blamed Germany for the war. So after Hitler took power, we could say 'Thank

God, now we have an army again, now we can put things right and get back the land that has been taken away from us'.

Others, though, saw the political imperative that fuelled the policies of Hitler and Nazi Germany from a different angle, as the workings of a dictatorship that punished dissension with death. Benedikt Sieb was one of them. He was a nineteen-year old apprentice in Hamburg when his life was changed by the Nazi diktat.

'My apprenticeship ended in 1941, after two years, not because of anything I had done, but because in the factory where I worked, someone had been discovered listening to English radio programmes. He was sentenced to death. I became involved because the Gestapo wanted me to make a statement as an eyewitness. I refused to do it. The next thing I knew, the Gestapo demanded that I sign up for the Russian front or they'd send me to a concentration camp and my parents would be shot. So I signed up.'

Rudolf Oelkers was in an even more invidious position, as the son of a social democrat. Democrats, socialists, communists, trades unionists and other political opponents had been the first targets of the Nazis after Hitler came to power in 1933. Many were imprisoned in concentration camps, many were executed. Oelkers' father was more fortunate: he was given a choice. Rudolf Oelkers still has the documents in which his father's choices were spelled out.

'My father was told: "Either you keep quiet or you'll be put into a concentration camp'. He decided not to go to the concentration camp, but he also decided not to keep quiet. We lived in a country village, so everyone knew about my father. It was very uncomfortable - probably dangerous - because and there were members of the SS in the village. Everyone knew me as 'the red', the 'communist' son of a 'communist' father. I wasn't the only one. There were many more, but for their own safety, maybe, they all joined up.

'I wanted to do the same. Fortunately, my father stopped me from volunteering the Waffen-SS. I was only sixteen and had no idea what the SS, the Waffen-SS or the whole Nazi business was going to mean. Eventually, I was in Russia with the 18th Tank Division, the division commanded by Colonel Guderian himself. But afterwards, I was glad we lost the war. Can you imagine what would have happened if Hitler had won?'

Heinz Friederich, who was born in 1928, was in uniform for only the last three months of the War, but he remembers very well how he was forced to enlist.

'We were suddenly told at school that we had to register voluntarily. We were put under duress, we weren't allowed to leave the room until we had signed up. Two or three weren't at all willing, but they were physically forced to sign by their relatives. Probably the relatives had been threatened with something bad. After it was all over, it was said that we had registered voluntarily, of our own free will. What a farce!'

There were subtler ways of binding recruits to the Nazi cause. Some might call it economic blackmail. However, before the War, Helmut Benzing, who trained for the Kriegsmarine, but ended up seeing the destruction and capture of Berlin in 1945, feels he had had good cause to be grateful for the generosity of the Nazi state and with that, good cause to serve it in war.

'I knew the time when unemployment was rife, so when the Nazis came and suddenly, my father got work and everyone got work, I was convinced it was for the best. We didn't know anything else, or rather what we did know wasn't good - hunger, unemployment and so on.

'We were very young, of course and we didn't have any contact with the outside world. We could only see and believe in what was happening in front of us. There was no television and no one who could tell you about different ways of doing things. Whether or not those ways - the Nazi ways - were right or wrong, we couldn't judge, that's the truth. I say again that we were much too young and we didn't hear any contrary opinions about what was going on with the Nazis.'

Leo Mattowitz, who served in Russia during the War, had also known some very hard times before Adolf Hitler came to power

'In 1933, when Hitler took power, I was eleven years old. In the Ruhrgebiet where I lived, there was abject poverty, I went to school with a small piece of bread, my father was out of work, everyone was out of work, it was a time of great poverty. We had no shoes, only clogs and I had to walk four kilometres to school even in the winter through the snow. I got my first shoes from Adolf Hitler. All of a sudden, my father was given work, the neighbours got work and I was delighted to wear proper shoes for the first time. So of course we all supported Hitler. He had rescued us from a terrible situation.'

What Mattowitz did not realise, as yet, was the even more terrible situation he was going to find when he was serving in Russia. Neither did another Russian veteran, Edmund Bonhoff, though he soon came to learn that once he was in the army there was no turning back.

'We grew up as Nazis. The Hitler Youth made us into Nazis. That was their whole aim. I was quite enthusiastic about the Hitler Youth. I was born in 1920, so I was thirteen when Hitler came to power - far too young to see all that Nazism really meant. Today, of course, I can see it differently, but then I know so much more. So much I wish I didn't know.

'Even so, I must say that we are all guilty, very guilty because of what the Nazis did. But the ordinary soldier as such, he just did his duty. All of us had to, because we'd have been punished otherwise. If any one of us had said 'We don't want to fight any more' or something like that, we'd have been shot immediately. We all knew that. We all knew about others who been shot. They did that often enough.'

Whatever the personal path that led them to war - whether it was duty or enthusiasm, whether they were pressured into it or believe their cause was just - for everyone, the Second World War a time of excitement and boredom, frantic action and waiting for action, facing death or escaping it, watching comrades die while others survived, and celebrating triumph or swallowing defeat. These German veterans saw it all and tell a sometimes fascinating, sometimes moving, often horrific tale of the long-ago war they fought and lost, but a war they can recall as if it happened yesterday.

Original caption: Even a hit like this on a dive bomber cannot harm a German airplane.

This was the most common German fighter of the war, over 35,000 were produced making the Me-109 the largest production run of any fighter on any side in World War II. Constantly upgraded between 1939 and 1945 the Me-109 remained operational until the very last days of the war. This excellent colour image shows of a pair of Me-109's on combat patrol in North Africa during 1942. The effectiveness of the desert camouflage pattern is suitably demonstrated by how well the machines blend in with the desert terrain.

THE BLITZKRIEG ERA
1939-1941

The blitzkrieg that exploded across Germany's border with Poland on 1st September 1939 was a new kind of warfare, more destructive, more terrifying, more shocking in its speed and power than any brand of fighting previously known. Overnight, other armies were made to look antiquated now that the forces of Nazi Germany had demonstrated for the first time what armour, tanks and aircraft could do when they acted in concert. The meaning of blitzkrieg - lightning war - was fully justified. As the hapless Poles soon discovered, blitzkrieg struck hard, it struck fast and it struck decisively.

The attack on Poland was the point at which the appeasement policy previously followed by Britain and France finally broke down. They had allowed the forces of Nazi Germany to march into the Rhineland in 1936. They had protested, but did nothing, in 1938 when Adolf Hitler announced the Anschluss: this union of Austria and Germany had been forbidden under the Treaty of Versailles at the end of the First World War. They had given in when Hitler demanded the Sudetenland of Czechoslovakia, ostensibly to protect the rights of the German minority there. They failed to react when, contrary to his word, Hitler absorbed the rest of Czechoslovakia into the German Reich in March 1939. At that juncture, Poland was the next obvious target on Hitler's list of territorial demands and Britain and France promised the Poles their support if they were attacked.

Two days after Hitler's forces invaded Poland and refused all demands to withdraw, Britain and France, together with Australia and New Zealand, declared war. By then, the Germans were well on their way to an easy victory and despite the promises, the Poles were left to fight on their own. The British, the French and the world could only watch as the German armoured columns sliced through Poland, backed by the Luftwaffe which plastered Polish airfields and destroyed runways, hangars and fuel stores. Railways and communication lines were systematically disrupted.

With no armoured divisions, few antitank or anti-aircraft weapons and a largely obsolete air force, the Polish army had scant chance. Enveloped by a double-double encirclement, Polish power to fight back was virtually eliminated and the last major Polish defence, at the battle of the Bzura River, ended with the surrender of 100,000 Poles. Although Warsaw managed to hold out until 27 September and the last organised resistance did not cease until 5

October, the Germans had prevailed in less than three weeks, by 19 September. Soviet Russia, then an ally of Nazi Germany, had invaded two days earlier and ultimately, Poland was dismembered and most of it was shared out between them.

Hajo Hermann, holder of the Knight's Cross with Swords, who later became a famous bomber ace, scoring nine victories, flew over the border with Poland on the first day of the invasion. The German forces, always the focus of Josef Goebbels' inventive propaganda department, had been told that they were making a defensive move: the Poles were going to invade Germany and so deserved to be attacked. Hajo Hermann, who was to become a famous night-fighter pilot, had his own ideas about that. He believed that the Poles had invited retribution through their ingratitude towards Germany after the First World War.

'We liberated Poland in the First World War. At the time, it was a province of Russia. We made it independent and said: 'You can have your kingdom again!' But were the Poles grateful? Not a bit of it! After the War, the Poles acted against us and took western Prussia away from us, and Upper Silesia. That was a very great injustice. When you think of 1 September 1939, you have to bear this in mind. When you flew against the Polish enemy remembering how they betrayed us, you feel very patriotic, there's no mistaking it. If nowadays, someone says: "How could you have done that? That's how the War began!' That's nonsense, nothing began on 1 September. The War started only when Britain and France declared war on us two days later.'

Hans Lehmann, who was with the invasion troops on the first day, had a less virulent view of the Poles.

'No. I didn't hate them. As far as I was concerned they were human beings, not that I loved them, you understand. It's simply that they were a foreign people, that's all, but I didn't feel that I had to exterminate them, or whatever, I can't say that. That was true of only a very few people. It's also true, though, that men become brutal when they are at war for too long, it gets easier and easier to shoot a person the longer you are out there''.

Strictly speaking, the German campaign in Poland was not true blitzkrieg. It was basically a conventional land war with certain blitzkrieg elements. Those elements were decisive, though. The most important was the element of surprise, which was why there was no formal declaration of war by Germany. As intended, the Poles were caught completely off guard. Hans Lehmann remembers how unprepared they were.

'The Poles hadn't expected to be invaded and we really did take them by surprise. We were able to just walk in at first. Then, the first troops arrived and by that time, the Poles knew what was happening. They started firing, but it wasn't very effective. In comparison to ours, the Polish weapons were so out of date that they couldn't do anything. We fired back, of course, and some of the Poles were shot. The others either ran away or surrendered. Afterwards, the whole Polish army realised they were helpless and capitulated'

Blitzkrieg theory had no place, either, for the preliminary artillery bombardment which had been regular practice before major battles in the First World War. Instead, the Germans delivered swift-striking attacks from the air. One of the Luftwaffe's major players was the Ju-87 'Stuka' dive bomber which had already shown its paces during the Spanish Civil War of 1936 to 1939, when it was used by the German Condor Legion to bring new and previously unimagined brand of terror to warfare. The Ju-87, capable of a top speed of 255 mph and armed with two 7.9mm MG81 and two 7.9mm MG17 machine guns, carried a bomb load of around 2,000 pounds, but it created panic and confusion on the ground even before any of these weapons came into play.

Ugly and angular, the Ju-87's gull-wings gave it a thoroughly sinister appearance. The dive-bombers swooped down like birds of prey, giving off a chilling screaming sound. This sound was produced by the sirens the Germans fitted to the wheel-covers. Colloquially, they were called the 'Trombones of Jericho', with all the promise of utter destruction that Biblical reference implied. Hans Lehmann remembers the effect as the Ju-87s dived on their victims below.

'The Stukas - they dived onto the enemy lines and the moral state of the adversary was so depressed because of the terrible sound it made. They had already begun to run the moment they heard it. They weren't going to wait for the bombs to fall!'

In Poland, tanks as well as aircraft, appeared in a new guise. Like the military aircraft, the tank had been a newcomer to war in 1914-1918, but the requirements of blitzkrieg had helped to transform it from the 'lozenge' designed to lumber across the muddy First World War terrain to the heavier, much more aggressive and speedy prime mover of the Second.

The tank and the Germans' use of it in Poland and afterwards, in western Europe, epitomised a long-held tenet of the Prussian military system: the value of mobility. The fighting in the First World War had been the antithesis of mobility and restoring it to its proper place in warfare played an important part in searching analysis undertaken after 1918 by Germany's keenest military minds. They were determined to avoid a repetition of the essentially phyrric nature of the first War, with its futile battles of attrition and costly effort for the sake of little gain. Never again, they resolved, would Germany be brought to her knees by a long-drawn out war or starved into submission by blockade. It was unthinkable, too, that the horrors of trench warfare should ever be repeated. Future wars were going to be aggressive, swift and decisive.

One of the most acute and perceptive of German military minds was Heinz Guderian, who became the legendary German tank commander of the Second World War. Guderian's aim was create large tank units that could range over the battlefield at will, causing maximum damage, doing it fast, and operating independently of infantry and other forces.

The future tank force, as Guderian saw it, would be concentrated in armoured divisions, not dispersed in small numbers. They would be spearheads of a single, large military formation which also included aircraft, artillery and mechanised infantry. Tank commanders would not remain in positions far in the rear, but would operate near the front, responding instantly to changing situations and issuing orders by radio directly to his units.

Making the most efficient use possible of available technology was only part of Guderian's plans. He also had a clear understanding of the value of proper training, and the fact that it was vital to encourage drive and initiative even in the lowest ranks. The German Army as a whole was an army of incomparable standards, but the men of the tank arm were to be trained to an even higher pitch of excellence.

Heinz Guderian was regarded as something of a maverick among the German 'top brass' and, as he stated in his memoirs, his concept of warfare was too revolutionary for the ultra-conservative General Staff. As a result, Guderian claimed, they blocked his ideas for many years. All the same, in the late 1930s, Guderian's theories appealed where it mattered most in Nazi Germany: the Führer himself approved.

Adolf Hitler had his own, political, use for swift, decisive war as envisaged by Guderian and others of like mind. During the late 1930s, Hitler appeared to be just a cynical risk-taker, dangling British and French politicians like puppets and relying on their fear of another war to force territorial gains out of them. This did not mean he was unaware of realities. If he were to make his strike in his long-planned strike in eastern Europe, then he would have to do it quickly. If he waited, Britain and France could become too strong for him and there might never be another opportunity.

The chance Germany would be taking in another war was already known even outside Germany, as Georg Lehrmann discovered when he heard a chilling prediction from a Czech prisoner. The prediction was remarkably accurate, and the Czech's conclusion was that Germany would lose.

'In Czechoslovakia, we were based in a small town ten kilometres from the German border. We had a Czech prisoner who spoke perfect German, so that we were able to converse very easily. He told us 'Listen ,you can start a war with us, but don't start on the others because then you have had it'. I said 'How

Engine torn from its supports by airscrew out of balance owing to a hit, and hanging only from the drag wires. The airplane flew home with the other two engines.

is that possible?' and he replied, 'I know it. First of all, you'll probably march on France and then on Russia and then you'll get it in the neck.' That is what the Czech said before the war had even begun.'

The Czech prisoner was, of course, right about Russia. What he could not take into account was the extent to which blitzkrieg was going to move the goal posts of warfare. For a start, the Luftwaffe first purpose was to seize control of the air. To do that, they would destroy the Polish air force on the ground. Although some Polish planes escaped - they had been moved to new locations - the Luftwaffe succeeded in virtually annihilating the rest after only two days, by 3rd September. This was the first demonstration in the Second World War of a truism: the fact that superiority in the air was the ultimate superiority. From then on, what little hope the Poles might have had vanished completely.

Once the German air force had taken care of the preliminaries, the tanks and other armoured units moved in and sliced a swathe of destruction across Poland, the like of which had never been seen in war before. Hitler himself was astonished by the havoc when he visited the tank corps soon after the invasion.

A communiqué issued by the Germans at this time was naturally triumphalist in tone, but at the same time, largely accurate:

'in a series of battles of extermination, of which the greatest and most decisive was in the Vistula curve, the Polish army numbering one million men has been defeated, taken prisoner or scattered. Not a single Polish active or reserve division, not a single independent brigade, has escaped this fate. Only fractions of single bands escaped immediate annihilation by fleeing into the marshy territory in eastern Poland. There, they were defeated by Soviet troops. Only in Warsaw, Modlin and on the peninsula of Hela in the extreme north of Poland are there still small sections of the Polish army fighting on and these are in hopeless positions.'

However futile the Germans considered their position to be, the manner in which some Poles fought back was savage. Hans Lehmann was an eyewitness.

'There was hand to hand fighting in Poland, man against man. The were fanatics on both sides. It's either you or it's me and to the death, they were saying. Forget about being taken prisoner. You feel hatred perhaps for a moment if someone has been shot beside you, you feel great hatred of the opponent...'

Individual reprisals were not unusual. Hans Lehmann became involved in one such incident after a young Pole was arrested.

'A company commander said to me 'He had a knife on him, you must shoot him!' A Polish man, a young Polish man, he could have been only about twenty-one years old. Because I had known the commander for some time, I said 'You're off your head. I won't do it'. Fortunately, I got away with it because I knew him. If it had been an officer I didn't know, then he would have shot me straight away. Experiences like this made me very, very sad. But then, for us it was to a greater or lesser extent depressing anyway. Some men, young men mostly, took it all quite lightly, but others took it very badly. Some of our comrades, when it began in Poland, actually messed their pants'.

Eventually, after some three weeks, the battle for Poland resolved itself into a last desperate struggle for the capital, Warsaw. For a long time, the defenders refused all demands to surrender and were subjected to day after day of bombing and shelling. By 26th September, it was reported that the city's business centre was in flames. Over a thousand civilians were reported killed, and four churches and three hospitals filled with wounded were destroyed. According to the German communiqué, there were no longer any buildings in Warsaw remaining intact, and not a house in which there had not been a victim of bombs or shells. Within the previous twenty-four hours some hundred fires had broken out following the launching of a hail of incendiary bombs.

On 21 September, six days before the surrender of Warsaw, the city's Lord Mayor, M. Starzynski, issued his own statement. It was a bitter comment on what the Nazis had labelled 'a humanitarian war'.

'I want the whole civilised world to know what the Nazi Government means by humanitarian war. Yesterday, in the early hours of the morning, seven of our hospitals were bombed, among many other buildings, with terrible results. Soldiers wounded on the battlefield were killed in their beds. Many civilians, among them women and children, were killed outright or buried under the ruins. But the most barbaric crime was committed against the Red Cross Hospital, which had the Red Cross flags flying from the windows. Several hundred wounded Polish soldiers were there.'

Despite brave words and the defiance of Warsaw, many Poles yielded to the logic of the situation without too much of a struggle. Hans Lehmann belonged to a platoon that was put in charge of four hundred Polish prisoners.

'They were glad the war was over for them. It all happened so fast that they were completely overrun before they knew it. You see, if a man realises there's no prospect of changing a situation, then he surrenders, he wants to protect his life.'

Similarly, on the march into Poland, Lehmann passed through whole villages where there was no appreciable resistance.

'If a village didn't have any soldiers, then the men didn't bother to take up arms. There was one village now and again where we were fired at but on the whole, the civilian population remained very calm, in order to protect their property and possessions. They knew that at the moment when foreign soldiers arrive, it could cost them their lives if they rebelled against them'.

Polish resistance nevertheless cost the Germans dear, both in men and materiél. They lost more men in Poland than in their later campaigns in the Norway, the Low Countries, France and the Balkans. put together. According to Hans Lehmann, the casualties had begun at the border on the first day.

'When we marched into Poland, there were corpses all around. Many of them were Germans. They lay around and no one bothered about them. I was so upset that couldn't eat for three days. Later on, almost the whole company was destroyed, and our armoured cars, too. If they'd been put out of action, we had to leave them. If the caterpillar tracks were hit, then you were unable to move even if the whole vehicle hadn't been destroyed. Some of the caterpillar tracks were blown clean off, so you couldn't drive any more. On one occasion, there were ten or eleven of us together with a second driver. They were all injured - and very badly - except for me.'

The German triumph in Poland was so speedy that, ironically, it made trouble for Lehmann. His platoon was ordered to take their four hundred Polish prisoners to Danzig and then rejoin their unit. It did not work out that way.

'We couldn't get back, so instead, we returned to our headquarters in Harburg. The next thing we knew, we were being threatened with a Court Martial as deserters! It was all sorted out in the end, but the reason we hadn't been able to follow orders and rejoin our unit was that the campaign in Poland was over so quickly. Before we could catch up with them, our unit had moved out and returned to Germany!'

After Poland, hostilities on land settled down what contemporary journalists termed the Phony War or, among the Germans, the Sitzkrieg or Twilight War. Sitzkrieg did not mean inactivity, but there two important factors governed this outwardly quiet time that was so much of a contrast to the shock and drama of the Polish campaign.

The first was the defensive attitude of the French. The German High Command feared the military strength of France and had objected, for example, to Hitler's reoccupation of the Rhineland in 1936 in case this prompted the French to use this strength against them. When France, with Britain had declared war on Germany, they had been appalled at the idea of confronting this mighty power they fancied lay across their western frontier. What they did not take sufficiently into account was that the French military concept of the time was predominantly defensive. During the Phony War period, they confined their operations to occasional patrols, a few probing missions and intelligence forays, but basically, they sat behind their much-vaunted Maginot Line awaiting events.

The Germans, for their part, held back from attacking the French at this juncture because they had only 23 divisions on their western frontier to France's one hundred. The rest of the German Army had been used in Poland

and time was needed to deploy and refit their forces for future action. However, future action, when it came, did not occur in the direction the troops had come to believe. Reinhold Runde of the Luftwaffe air signal corps was one of many who believed that the next target of attack would be Britain.

'We all had the feeling after the Polish campaign that we would be going to England. All of us in the Luftwaffe though we'd be off to England one way or another. no one dreamed that it would Denmark and Norway'.

At that time, Norway and Denmark were neutral, but their geographical position posed a danger to the vital supplies of iron ore that came to German north coast ports from Sweden. The route for these supplies ran from Narvik, the ice-free port on Ofotfjord, through the Norwegian Leads and on to Germany. The Royal Air Force, flying from Britain, could easily disrupt this supply line, so that securing the two Scandinavian countries under German control became imperative.

Norway had particular attractions, with its long coastline indented by a mass of fjords. In German hands, that coastline could help prevent the chance of a British blockade, deny Britain control of the trade routes and put a stop to any threat they could pose by occupying bases there.

The Danes were the first victims of this next German campaign. Denmark was invaded, though not yet formally occupied, on 9 April 1940. It was all over within a day. The Wehrmacht met nominal resistance from the Danish Royal Guard before the Germans took charge and Luftwaffe aircraft circling overhead obliged a very reluctant King Christian X to co operate. King Haakon VII of Norway was made of sterner stuff. He refused the German demand to accept a government led by the collaborator Vidkun Quisling and with his ministers, resolved to resist.

By then, the German land, sea and air invasion was already under way.

On 7th April, the same day the British decided, after much hesitation, to mine the Norwegian Leads, Reinhold Runde was on board ship as vehicles from the air intelligence battalion and flak guns were being loaded into the holds.

'Another ship anchored in front of us was loaded with dismantled plane sections, flak and artillery, also with flak and artillery. The next night, we were instructed that we had to leave the deck, and go below because we were about to sail through sovereign Danish waters between the Danish islands in order to get to the Skagerrak.'

These precautions were necessary because Denmark was still neutral and uninvaded at that juncture, though not of course, for long, and the German ships had to avoid detection by the Danes. They were lucky.

'Though they prowled around, the Danes didn't notice that the ships were loaded with war material. Merchant ships often sailed this route and I suppose they assumed that ours were the same. It was only when we had left sovereign Danish waters in the direction of Skagerrak that we were able to stop and get together with the rest of the invasion fleet: thirteen heavy transport ships, torpedo boats and minesweepers. We had to be careful of mines, so one ship sailed behind the other with the mine sweepers and torpedo boats between them.

'In the early morning hours on 9th April, we saw in front of us, approaching from the west, the heavy cruiser Blücher, which was supposed to be unsinkable, and the small cruiser Emden. We were in the second ship behind the Blücher and we were able to see that there were nurses and heavy flak on the deck. At around 0500 hours, the convoy slowly got under way. Just before we entered Oslo Fjord, all the ships were stopped, and torpedo boats drew up alongside each one and handed the ship's officers a document roll.'

Runde and his comrades were about to be informed that they were going to occupy Norway as friends, not enemies. The author of this fiction was Adolf Hitler.

'We were all ordered out on deck. The Führer's orders were read to us, saying that we had to occupy Norway as a protection for the Norwegians - and ourselves - against Britain and France. In case the Norwegians didn't under stand this, and tried to resist, they had to be crushed without consideration. And so we sailed on into the Oslo Fjord. The entrance to the fjord was very wide, with Sweden on one side Norway on the other.

'Then suddenly, the Blücher started firing shells towards the shore, but we couldn't see exactly where they were aimed. At that moment, some tactical Luftwaffe aircraft roared over our heads in the dawn light, heading towards Norway. All of a sudden, there was an explosion on the Blücher and we saw clouds of smoke.'

What this meant was Britain was coming to the aid of the Norwegians and the Royal Air Force had arrived. The fourth ship behind Runde's was hit, with devastating consequences for the Germans on board.

'Before we sailed into Oslo Fjord, three British torpedo planes had come over and bombed a German tanker, the fourth ship behind us. The tanker was hit by torpedoes and sank, leaking its oil over the water. The sea caught fire - we saw it burning - and we heard men screaming and screaming, such horrible screams! It wasn't possible to save them, that was evident. No-one from the German fleet, neither the navy command nor anyone else, took any notice of the men swimming in the oil or attempted to rescue them. The order was straight ahead, straight ahead, straight ahead.

'We continued sailing, and we could still hear the heard the Blücher's guns firing. But clouds of smoke were belching out Blücher was going down. The ship was listing to port and soldiers were jumping off the decks into the sea. Before long, we saw Blücher sinking at the bows and gradually take everything and everyone left on board down into the depths. Soldiers were swimming on the surface, the temperature of the water was below freezing point at the time'.

Blücher had been hit by 11.2 inch and 6-inch guns fired from the shore and although her captain, Heinrich Woldag managed to get her anchored onshore in hopes of repairing her turbines, successive explosions defeated the effort. Blücher had to be abandoned at 0700 hours and at 0723, she capsized and sank. Reinhold Runde watched.

'We noticed a low throbbing noise in the ship, several throbbing noises. We knew something was wrong and we were all up on the deck. Suddenly, Blücher was firing again. We saw muzzle flashes from her starboard side. She was firing towards the Oslo Fjord, but she had started to list to port. We saw soldiers and also nurses sliding down the deck into the Oslo Fjord, the list was so pronounced that they could no longer hold on and it didn't take long before we saw that the stern of the Blücher rising up into the air. The bow was pressed downwards.

'At that moment, German tactical planes roared over our heads and bombed fortifications to our left which turned out to be the Oskarsborg fortifications. We didn't know it then, but the fortress was armed with torpedo emplacements. The exterior of Oskarsborg was quite badly damaged, we could see that. Several waves of planes flew in but during this raid by German planes the Blücher was sinking more and more, and then disappeared, bow first into Oslo Fjord. It happened quite quickly. It was certainly all observed from both the Swedish and Norwegian shores because shortly afterwards, fishing boats came out and tried to save the men swimming around in the water.

'More and more of them arrived. Our ships were now stationary, beside the sinking Blücher, waiting for the rescue to begin. No one from our ship took part in the rescue operation, it was all done by civilians, Norwegians and Swedes. The Swedish Navy also came out with ships and searched for survivors. There were rocks sticking out of the water, and some of the people from Blücher tried to cling to them. But they were so slippery that they couldn't get a hand-hold and slid into the water and drowned. Some were saved in the last minute by the Norwegians and Swedes.'

There was nothing to do now but sail on towards Oslo. But the Blücher was given one last salute by the German ships.

'After this terrible disaster, all soldiers were assembled on deck, standing to attention as we sailed over the sunken Blücher towards Oslo. It all went smoothly. The Norwegians didn't attack and we reached Oslo without trouble.'

Meanwhile, the Wehrmacht's artillery units had gone ashore and fought

Rapidly flying, the Stuka has rushed downward; the bomb has just been released and will hit the mark in a few seconds.

their way into the Norwegian capital as far as the city's airport. The Norwegian planes parked there had been destroyed from the air and Luftwaffe bombers had landed on the runway. One of the German pilots was Hajo Hermann, whose war almost ended then and there.

'We had been sent to Norway because the British had landed a corps in Bergen and it was our job to attack their landing areas and support ships. When we arrived, we found the airfield was stuffed full with German planes. Then, I spotted one runway that was relatively clear. I flew in - I had a lot of bombs on board - and touched down but then the plane rolled and rolled and rolled. Either the runway was too short or I did it wrong. Anyway, our plane smashed into this narrow path at the end of the strip. My crew leaped out in a tremendous fright, but I stayed sitting in the plane and they screamed, ' You're going to explode! You're going to explode! Get out of there!' However, my mood was that of a ship's captain who wanted to go down with his ship. Fortunately, there was no explosion, but it was a very nasty moment for me.'

After Reinhold Runde's ship had berthed at Oslo, the vehicles were unloaded. The reception the Germans received as they drove through the capital was muted.

'The people of Oslo stood on both sides of the street and followed the passing convoys with their eyes. No shots were fired, we were able to march safely through. Some of the Norwegians even waved to us. They didn't seem all that angry and there was no resistance, but their faces were serious. We supposed that the radio stations had been taken over by Quisling who ordered the Norwegians to remain calm.'

From Oslo, the convoy drove to Hamar. Several of the vehicles had crews of ten, all armed with rifles and machine guns. The country was mountainous and the German vehicles proved to be too wide and too high for the narrow roads, so progress was slow. The convoy passed through wooded country and the Germans were fired on by Norwegian soldiers hidden in the trees. No one was hit, Runde remembers, but the Germans prepared to fight back.

'We got out of our vehicles now and again and set up firing positions. But we hardly saw an adversary, there was snow and ice everywhere, everything was covered, the passes and the roads too. Sometimes we had get out and shovel snow before we could drive on'.

The task assigned to Runde's unit was to repair telephone lines to airports and command posts. When they reached Trondheim, where the lines had been damaged by the Norwegians, the two German battle cruisers Scharnhorst and Gneisenau were in harbour after participating in the German landings at Narvik. During the War, the British made several attempts to destroy the battle cruisers to stop them preying on Allied convoys in the Atlantic. Gneisenau survived the War, but Scharnhorst was destroyed by naval action in 1943. Three years earlier Rienhold Runde, witnessed an early British attempt to sink the commerce raiders which were such a danger to them.

'Two days after we arrived in Trondheim, there was a British air raid on the Scharnhorst and Gneisenau. Scharnhorst was slightly damaged by bombs exploding on deck, a gun-barrel was smashed and the decking suffered damage. Three days later, we sailed from Trondheim and visited the two ships. Our job in the signal corps was to inspect the air raid damage and make an official report.'

Runde and the rest of the signal corps moved on to Steinkier, and along the way, witnessed the Luftwaffe and the Royal Air Force in action.

'Now and again during our journey from Trondheim to Steinkier, British planes flew over Trondheim Fjord and were fought off by German fighters, Some were shot down, and British soldiers who had landed north of the Trondheim fjord were captured down, and were captured by the Germans. They were taken to the fortifications at Trondheim where they were treated as German POW's according to the provisions of the Geneva Convention.'

Runde remembers ruefully how well these British prisoners were treated compared to their German counterparts.

'They were sent packets from England. They were allowed to buy food. They had regular postal contact and cards from the International Red Cross. These prisoners even received civilian visitors and had visits from other captured British units. That was all possible for them, but it was denied to us Germans in other countries during the War.'

When the Norwegians finally surrendered, on 9th June 1940, Runde's unit was in Namsos, which had been evacuated by British forces several weeks earlier, on 3rd May. The Norwegian army was allowed to hand in their weapons, remove their uniforms if they wished to and then went home, or rather they were supposed to go home. Having lost the regular war, many later resorted to irregular warfare and became partisans. Reinhold Runde encountered them.

'There were Norwegian soldiers up in the mountains. They fired at us and we only saw them as they ran off across the snow and ice amongst the trees. We had to get out of our cars, use them as cover and then fire our rifles. I myself carried the P38 submachine gun. Our cars were quite heavily armoured, a rifle bullet wouldn't have penetrated them and the Norwegians were firing rifles, rather old-fashioned rifles as we later discovered. They had long barrels and looked like weapons we had seen in museums. I think they came from the First World War. The Norwegians didn't have modern weapons, like the latest machine-guns. They used water-cooled MGs and they were ineffective.'

By the time the Norwegians surrendered, another fighting front had been opened up by blitzkrieg, this time in western Europe when the Germans invaded Belgium, the Netherlands, Luxembourg and France on 10th May 1940. This was the blitzkrieg which obliged the British to finally withdraw their troops from Norway and return home to defend their own country. King Haakon and the Norwegian royal family went with them and spent the rest of the War as exiles in Britain. From there, Haakon, an exemplary monarch provided the inspiration for the Norwegian resistance to the Germans.

The blitzkrieg in the west was a shock, despite the first demonstration in Poland. The shock had an extra edge because the Germans did what many military experts had considered impossible. The Maginot Line had stood as an impregnable barrier on the Franco-German border ever since it was completed in 1935 after five years' construction. The gap where in ended in the north, at the Belgian frontier, was covered by the Ardennes forest, a plateau up to 500 metres above sea level and so thick with trees that it was considered impassable. For that reason, the Ardennes region was weakly defended. On 10th May, the impregnable barrier was outflanked and the impassable forest was penetrated as the German armour crashed through.

The French, had neglected this region, mainly because they were relying on the massive fortifications of the Maginot Line. The Germans had to contend with little more than a bemused Belgian cavalryman, who peered uncomprehendingly through the trees. Once clear of the Ardennes, the German blitzkrieg surged through the Netherlands and Belgium and within four days, the Dutch had surrendered, followed a fortnight later, on 28th May, by Belgium.

The Germans had devised this strategy, not only as a means of entering western Europe in force and by surprise, but as a feint, designed to draw the British and French northwards, away from their entrenched defensive positions in France. Meanwhile, the Luftwaffe was in action, unleashing devastating bombing raids on key targets in Holland and German paratroopers landed both north and south of the Hague.

An English newspaper reporter was in The Hague when the attack began.

'Just as dawn was breaking, hundreds of aircraft came over the city and bombs were falling everywhere. The sky seemed to be filled with planes and parachute troops were being dropped in large numbers on several parts of the city. Meanwhile, the bombers concentrated their efforts on the important buildings, including the barracks.

'When the smoke and dust had subsided, I saw that several buildings, including the prison, had been destroyed. Bombers accompanied by fighters came over in waves of two hundred at a time, some as low as 250 metres above the ground. While I watched, Dutch anti-aircraft guns bagged six large machines. One, a forty-seater troop carrier, burst into flames, struck another and both came down. They destroyed three houses and I saw forty or fifty bodies in the street.

'At the same time, seaplanes with detachable rubber pontoons, each containing forty men, sailed on the shallow water near the shore. Five hundred men were landed on the beach in this way, wading ashore from the pontoons.

'Each parachute party numbered about forty, in charge of a sergeant. These men took the town hall, museum and library near the square. A civilian defence corps, armed only with butchers' knives was formed immediately to counteract the parachutists.'

George Lehrmann's unit virtually walked in when they were sent across the Dutch-Belgian border.

'We just marched over Belgium, the Albert canal, to the English Channel. It was no problem. The Albert Canal had been taken by parachute units. They jumped out backwards from gliders. They couldn't do that carrying rifles, so they had small 25-round machine-guns strapped to their stomachs'.

Driving on into France, the Germans encountered their first considerable obstacle in the River Meuse. The river was reached on the morning of 13th May and the plan was to cross it at three points. To ensure that the crossing was not interrupted, nearby Sedan, sited on the river near the Belgian frontier, was subjected to an intensive bombardment lasting six hours. After this murderous onslaught, Guderian's engineers crossed the Meuse swiftly, followed by the first of the German infantry.

That same evening, the Germans smashed their way over the river and were on the opposite bank in strength. The French defenders, shattered by the onslaught, were unable to stop them. Both the other crossing were successfully forced, and the defence was in tatters.

The Low Countries and northern France offered ideal tank country, stretching out flat and even for miles on end. The defenders, mainly ill-equipped and elderly reservists, were no match for the surge of blitzkrieg power that overwhelmed them. The Luftwaffe's dive-bombers were already at work, wreaking wholesale destruction and inspiring widespread terror. But there was more to come. Behind the spearheads extending back from the River Meuse there were twenty-five divisions of supporting infantry.

By 16th May, the southern French defences were gaping wide and it was evident that a potential catastrophe was in the making. The Luftwaffe had command of the air, easily repulsing attempts to bomb German targets. The bombing of Abbeville was typical of the blanket destruction wrought by blitzkrieg from the air. Alan Stuart Roger of the Red Cross organisation saw what happened.

One of the dive bombers came too close to the water when pulling out during an attack on coastal fortifications, whereby it lost the whole undercarriage and the airscrew was slightly bent. In that condition the machine returned in formation to the base airdrome more than 120 km off and landed smoothly on the underside of the fuselage.

'Abbeville became one vast desolation of smouldering ruins, fires raging and the shattered streets strewn with dead and dying women and children. The Germans bombed it relentlessly, without any thought of military objectives. They dropped high explosive and incendiary bombs, as well as incendiary darts, which shoot about like jumping crackers.

'I saw a house where a delayed-action bomb, ricocheting from the ground, flew clean through the bedroom in which a man and his wife were asleep. By a thousand one chance, the missile landed harmlessly outside. But wherever there was a jam on the road, the Luftwaffe swooped down, bombing and machine-gunning the processions of fugitives.'

On 21st May, German forces broke through to the Channel coast, capturing Arras, Amiens as well as Abbeville. The French managed to retrieve Arras next day, but their air force was nowhere to be seen. The French had hundreds of aircraft, but they had been removed to safe locations and were unavailable for action. The shattered French armies, literally knocked backwards by the Germans' blitzkrieg power, attempted to make a hasty retreat from the lowlands but found the roads clogged with panic-stricken refugees. Meanwhile, the twin German spearheads were thrusting on, driving deeper and deeper into France.

Many Germans involved in this helter-skelter advance were exhilarated by it, but not all. War and its ugly sights were still new to many of the younger soldiers and they were emotionally affected by it. Herbert Boehm saw what happened when a French tank was destroyed.

'A French tank was shot into flames, and the tank commander got out of the burning machine. As he came into view out of the turret, he was shot, killed by one of the bullets flying all around him. No one actually aimed at him, but he was hit just the same. He toppled to the ground, dead. It shocked me, I can tell you. He thought he was going to save himself, but he was killed instead!'

Guderian's tanks raced from the River Meuse to the sea in an astounding sweep that exemplified blitzkrieg in its purest and most lethally efficient form. Guderian was impatient and the exhilaration of this swift drive to the sea brought out all his impetuosity. At Guderian's urging, the Panzers frequently covered more than 80 kms. a day, far outstripping the infantry and causing acute alarm among his superiors. Quite often, the mere sight of the thundering tanks eating up the distance was enough to make the opposition move out of the way, and fast. For the Germans, it was like a joy-ride.

Guderian and his tanks were the stuff of which legends were made and legends were rapidly made in France in the summer of 1940. All over the country, even in places far away from the northern battlefield, wild rumours circulated about Fifth Columnists and saboteurs who had betrayed the forces -

and the honour - of France and delivered them up into the power of the merciless invaders. Gossips whispered about German paratroops, strangely disguised, and further terrible disasters soon to occur.

These rumours both sprang from and further encouraged the rather defeatist French cast of mind. This attitude had already been evident in the First World War. Twenty years later, the gloom that settled over them as their land was gobbled up by the Germans brought it to the surface. It did not seem to matter now that the French had more troops than the invaders, and even more tanks, or that the best of them, such as the heavily armed Chars and Soumas were formidable weapons of war in their own right. None of this counted where the will to use this military strength was lacking, as it was in France in 1940. To make matters even worse, if that were possible, the French and British Allies were indulging in petty squabbles and inter-service rivalries, weakening even further their will to resist. Rarely, if ever, in war had defenders found themselves in such a dire state of helplessness and disarray.

The French, nevertheless, resisted desperately, even though they were outclassed. George Lehrmann fought against them in the front line:

'The French fought partly from trenches, but it wasn't the trench fighting of twenty years before. In 1940, when soldiers moved forward, they went in waves, not lines. The First War was a war of man against man. There was some of that in the Second, but it was much more a war of machines. We were motorised, we had armoured cars. Well, they weren't really armoured cars, they had just 3 mm of metal. On top we had a 2 cm cannon and machine guns, and men fired from those moving vehicles, too. Of course, the attack took place over quite a wide distance but it wasn't disproportionately wide, the front line, not like in the First World War. Mostly, we were the ones who attacked. The French fired back of course, but German superiority was too great. The French apparently, hadn't expected it. We also had larger amounts of weaponry than the French.

'We had relatively few casualties, and of course, we had marvellous support from the Luftwaffe. Our JU-87 Stukas terrified the French just as they had terrified the Poles in 1939. I suppose that when you're already tense and anxious, and thinking you're going to be killed any moment, the screaming of the Stukas is enough to put you over the edge. Many soldiers simply ran away as if banshees were after them.

'I've got to admit, though, that I was frightened, too. Not by the Stukas, of course. They were on our side. It was the whole business of fighting and killing and dying that frightened me. I never trembled so much in my entire life as when we went into the fighting. I sometimes felt I was frozen with fear.

'We saw terrible things, really terrible. I remember once that we were involved in fighting and were camouflaged under some brushwood when we

Original caption: Observer and pilot over Norway

34

saw a French plane shot down. The plane spiralled downwards and then suddenly it twisted around and dropped down right onto one of our vehicles. The noise, the flames, the smoke..... in a flash, the vehicle and its crew were gone. It was very hard to see that kind of thing, but there's always that selfish gratitude you feel that it didn't happen to you. It might have done, you know. The vehicle that was destroyed was only about 100 metres away.

'We couldn't do anything. It was too late for help. In a few moments, it was all burned out, just a mass of twisted metal. And the fighting was still going on around us. When that happens, all you can do is keep your head down. First rule in war - when there's a bang, get down fast, lightning fast; the one who got down fastest had the greatest chance of survival.'

By 20th May, after only ten days, Guderian's tanks had reached Amiens and the last link between the defenders in the north and the south was severed. The same day, the Germans captured Abbeville, and by 23rd May, all the ports on the English Channel were in their hands. Three days after that, in London, planning for Operation Dynamo, the evacuation of the British Expeditionary Force from France, was set in train.

The task could not have been more monumental. What had to be done was to lift 45,000 men from the beaches, jetties and piers of Dunkirk and sail them home to Britain. In the event, the figure, which included French and Belgian soldiers, rose more than eight times over, to 338,000. At this juncture, an extraordinary and still controversial situation had intervened to give the British some hope that they could pull off this extraordinary feat. On 24th May, Adolf Hitler issued the order for Guderian's tanks to halt at the Dunkirk pocket and allow the Luftwaffe to finish off the British. The SS Liebstandarte Adolf Hitler, of the Waffen-SS, commanded by Sepp Dietrich, were in position on the Aa Canal southeast of Dunkirk. Dietrich ordered his men to ignore Hitler's order. They captured the Watten Heights on the opposite side at Dunkirk and were told to go into the attack. However, even this élite was unable to interfere with the effect of the 'Halt' order. The pause gave the British two days to complete their escape. Even though some of the heat was off, the Germans did not make it easy for them. George Lehrmann, who was there, recalls that Dunkirk was still a place where many soldiers lost their lives and never went home.

'We arrived at Dunkirk where the English were trying to escape. They took everything that was able to float - big naval ships, small yachts, small boats - and took off. We were able to pick up all the chocolate and cigarettes they had left behind. We stayed in Dunkirk for about thirty-six hours. Our guns were trained on the fleeing soldiers, who couldn't defend themselves any more, and we fired on them like crazy. I've often wondered why we did so. They wanted to get away, so what was it all about? When we'd finished, the Stukas arrived and thundered into the crowds of men on the beaches.'

One of the private shipowners who went to Dunkirk to help in the rescue described the German bombardments:

'On the afternoon of 30th May, when we got there, the German planes were coming over all the time. German troops couldn't have been very far away because they opened fire every now and then, and the shells would fall amongst our men. The aircraft came over from a northerly direction, eight or nine in a line, and so low that we could distinguish their markings quite plainly. They were using tracer bullets. Our men took cover and fired back with their rifles.

'On Saturday 1st June, the Germans started bombing attacks on the ships. At first, we were fairly lucky. Then another wave of bombers came over one after the other in a line, and they hit us. We soon had a very bad list, so we had to abandon ship and take to the boats. We kept the AA gun going all the time and as the ship was going down, our fellows were firing the pom-poms.

'Unfortunately, most of our boats had been wrecked in the attack and most of us had to take to the water. I swam away and managed to get onto a raft, where several others joined me. The Germans hadn't done with us yet, for they came back while a tug was taking men off the forecastle. They bombed the tug and all the men had to swim for it and get picked up again. Some climbed onto a wreck, but the Germans saw them and came back and bombed them there, too. There must have been hundreds of planes which kept returning again and again and when they had sunk the ships, they still weren't satisfied, but would bomb us again after we had been rescued.'

Vice-Admiral Bertram Ramsey, commander of the naval forces from Dover that went to the relief of Dunkirk, was just as graphic.

'The Germans sent over hordes of bombers, literally hundreds. They made Dunkirk docks a shambles. The whole place was son fire, and the heat was great that no troops could come down to the docks.

'We had to make alternative arrangements, or else we could not get any men away. The only part of Dunkirk harbour where a ship could go alongside was a narrow pier or breakwater of wooden piles. Eventually, there came something like 250,000 men off this pier, a place never intended in wildest imagination for a ship to go alongside and perform such a task.'

The task was certainly monumental. There were no gangways, and narrow mess tables were put across the planks from the pier to the ships. The soldiers 'walked the plank' to safety, mainly in the dark and most of them were so tired that they hardly drag their legs. In one day, 66,000 men were taken off the pier.

The Germans did everything they could to stop the evacuation. First, they mounted heavy batteries commanding the direct route to England passing near Calais. The British diverted to a new route, even though it meant that a 76-mile

Original caption: He-111 takes on fuel.

journey became a voyage of 175 miles. The Germans promptly brought up artillery batteries commanding this second route, and a third had to be found which had never been used before. Not surprisingly, either. The third route was obstructed by sandbanks which had to be swept and marked by buoys before it could be used.

On 4th June, Prime Minister Winston Churchill reported to the House of Commons:

'The Germans attacked on all sides with great strength and fierceness, and their main power, the power of their far more numerous air force, was thrown in to the battle, or else concentrated upon Dunkirk and the beaches.

'For four or five days, an intense struggle reigned. All their armoured divisions, together with great masses of German infantry and artillery, hurled themselves in vain upon the ever-narrowing, ever-contracting appendix within which the British and French armies fought.

'Meanwhile, the Royal Navy, with the help of countless merchant seamen, strained every nerve to embark the British and Allied troops. Two hundred and eighty light warships and 650 other vessels were engaged. They had to operate upon the difficult coast, often in adverse weather, under an almost ceaseless hail of bombs, and an increasing concentration of artillery fire.

'Meanwhile, the Royal Air Force engaged the main strength of the German Luftwaffe and inflicted upon them losses of at least four to one.'

Despite the Luftwaffe, the German E-boats and U-boats out in the Channel, the magnetic mines, and the gunfire from the shore-based batteries which had Dunkirk harbour in range, the evacuation was completed in nine days, by 4th June. The exploit was greeted as if it were a triumph, even though Churchill warned: 'We must be very careful not to assign to this deliverance the attributes of a victory. Wars are not won by evacuation.'

The French, left to face the Germans alone, fought on for another two weeks but they were unable to contain the might of the blitzkrieg. German forces entered Paris, marching past gaunt, shocked Parisians, some of whom wept openly, on 14th June. Six days later, the French surrendered. Two days after that, the French signed a truce with Nazi Germany, but in the most humiliating circumstances. The signing took place in the same railway carriage in which the French had received the German surrender in 1918. Twenty-two years later, victors and vanquished even used the same table and the same chairs. Now, it was the turn of Britain, the last combat still free to do so, to stand alone against the might of Nazi Germany.

Once the battle of France, the 'six-week war' was over, Germans garrisoned in France began to enjoy some of the more hedonistic privileges of a soldier's life. Hans Lehmann remembers it as 'a lovely time'.

Original caption: The faithful board mechanic helps his pilot to adjust his parachute. In a few seconds the machine will taxi to the take-off.

'It was high summer by the time the fighting France ended. Afterwards, we were stationed in different parts of France. We lived in private houses, When we were stationed by the River Loire, there was another river called the Deloire. Nearby was a very peaceful village. It was beautiful, very beautiful, directly beside the water..'

Georg Lehrmann was stationed at Le Mans though, like Lehmann, he had only a limited time to enjoy himself.

'I was billetted in a beautiful chateau. It was really lovely, the area around Le Mans. There were lots of pretty girls, lots of wine, lots of fun. The sort of life soldiers dream about. It happened so quickly, too. The war in France had lasted only six weeks and then it was finished. Our troops had been good, damned good! But that fool Hitler soon spoiled it all. He wanted too much, didn't he?'

What Hitler wanted was what he had always wanted. He had said so as long before as 1923, in his Mein Kampf, the book he had written while he was in prison for subversive activities. Mein Kampf was much more than a book. It was a statement of intent and a major theme was lebensraum in the east, living space for the overcrowded German people. Like Kaiser Wilhelm II before him, Hitler coveted the huge resources of Russia and his hatred of communism added extra fuel to his ambitions.

The process of moving east had already started in Poland where the Poles were 'relocated' and their lands handed over to new German settlers. More often than not, 'relocation' was a euphemism for the concentration camp. Beyond Poland lay the vast expanses of Russia and by August 1940, German divisions were being transferred to Poland in preparation for the opening of a new, eastern, front. The German forces were frequently re-grouped to conceal their numbers and Georg Lehrmann and Hans Lehman were among the many thousands of soldiers who were obliged to leave behind the delights of France and march east.

First, though, Hitler had to secure the southern flank of his invasion forces. To this end, he made treaties with Bulgaria, Hungary and Romania. That was the easy part. All three had right-wing governments that were in tune with Hitler's own. They were only too pleased to join the Axis, the group of powers first formed with the 'Pact of Steel' concluded by Germany and Italy in 1936.

Japan joined the Axis in 1940 and the three Balkan countries, followed by Slovakia and Croatia subsequently enlarged the grouping.

Yugoslavia was all set to belong, too, and on 25th March 1941, the Yugoslav prime ministers and foreign minister signed an agreement with Germany in Vienna on behalf of the pro-German regent, Prince Paul. Riots followed, and two days later, the 17-year old King of Yugoslavia, Peter II, supported a military coup d'état which removed the Prince from power. The agreement with Germany was immediately rescinded. British Prime Minister Winston Churchill commented: 'The Yugoslav nation has found its soul.' They also invited their fate.

Hitler, infuriated, decreed that Yugoslavia was to be smashed 'with merciless brutality, in a lightning operation'. It was another opportunity for blitzkrieg. The Yugoslav capital, Belgrade, was heavily bombed on 6th April 1941 and the German forces swept through the Vardar region in the south. The Royal Yugoslav army was caught in a barely mobilised state, poorly dispersed to contain the onslaught. The result, as gleefully broadcast on German state radio, was inevitable.

'Some 50,000 men and eight Yugoslav generals have been captured by a single German division. The roads present a picture of a complete military rout. They are strewn with abandoned and broken-down tanks as well as rifles and machine-guns.'

Yugoslav resistance had been vigorous, but there was no doubt about the outcome. Within twelve days, Zagreb, Sarajevo and Skopje had fallen. On 13th April, Belgrade fell and three days later, the Yugoslavs surrendered. the Germans claimed to have captured twenty thousand prisoners and a large number of guns and other war matériel. King Peter, a close relative of the British Royal Family, fled with his government to London.

The rapid defeat and occupation of Yugoslavia left another country still implacably opposed to the Germans and their demands: Greece. Germany's Italian Allies were supposed to have taken care of the Greeks after their invasion of 28th October 1940, but fanatical Greek resistance impelled them into a humiliating retreat. As his forces floundered, the Italian Duce, Benito Mussolini, appealed to the Germans for help.

The Greeks knew very well that the forces of Nazi Germany, and their appetite for vengeance, made them a very different prospect from the Italians. They, too, called in aid, from Britain. Piraeas, the port of Athens, became a supply centre for the British forces and Hajo Hermann was ordered to lay mines at the entrance to the port to prevent them using it. Hermann's flight did not go accordingly to plan.

'We were stationed in Sicily and apart from the mines, I had loaded two bombs onto my plane. This I was actually not allowed to do. I was told to unload them, but I only pretended to do so and flew off with my squadron with the bombs still on board.

'We flew in low over the bay of Patras over Corinth. First, I dropped mines into the entrance, the rest of the squadron sprinkled their mines down too, and then I spiralled upwards and made a clean run in, to aim at this large 'tub' moored at the quayside. We didn't dive down but flew on a horizontal line, at

Original caption: Luftwaffe crewman dons his winter fight suit.

about 1,000 metres, not very high. The spotlights wove all around us and the flak was shooting quite wildly, but my navigator paid no attention. He looked through his glass and I made corrections according to his instructions until he had released both the 'forbidden' bombs.

'I took the plane down to make sure we'd been on target,and then a detonation wave rose up, so enormous that I just hung in the air completely unable to steer. I thought my plane was doomed. You can't imagine a more violent detonation. Later, I learned that the Royal Navy Admiral Sir Andrew Cunningham reported that the harbour was totally destroyed. 'It was an explosion of atomic dimensions,' he said.

'The British couldn't get into or out of the harbour because this one hit of ours sank 41,000 tonnes of shipping at one blow. How did that happen? It's very difficult to sink so much tonnage even in a whole year, but what we'd done was hit a transport ship full of ammunition.

'Everyone in the harbour seemed to be stunned. The flak stopped, the searchlights stopped turning, and I just floated calmly above it all and watched. There were explosions all along the quayside, because bombs that had already been unloaded detonated and flew across the harbour'.

'But there was one British soldier - I'd really like to find out his name - he was the only one who took up his gun, a 4 cm , and fired at me. He hit one of my engines. I realised that I was never going to get my aircraft back to Sicily, so decided instead to fly to the island of Rhodes on our remaining engine. We had loaded quite a lot of fuel for the return journey,so the plane was heavy and sank lower and lower until we were flying only 50 metres above the sea. All of a sudden, I saw these cliffs sticking up out of the water. I managed to cheat my way past them, and we decided to offload some of the fuel so that we could fly at a more reasonable height.

'Unfortunately, there was a fault in the system and we couldn't stop the fuel flowing out. By the time we reached the southern tip of Rhodes, our tanks were on their last drop. There was a layer of high-lying fog and I couldn't see anywhere to land. We were managing to fly at about 800 metres by this time. I wanted to make radio contact with the airport, but the Italians who were manning it had decamped because the English had bombarded it. We were able to see one of the wrecked Italian planes, a Savoia, still smouldering.

'The Italians had switched off the electricity supply, but luckily there was a German radio operator who had an emergency unit. He wound it up and gave me bearings. I came down through the clouds, not flying, but gliding, and managed to land. The needle was at zero. We didn't have a drop of fuel left.'

The German invasion of Greece took place on the same day, 6th April 1941 as the invasion of Yugoslavia. It also proceeded in the same way. Two German corps stormed into northern Greece from Bulgaria, followed on 8th April by the Second Panzer division. This new blitzkrieg soon proved to be unstoppable. The Germans drove speedily towards the south, driving the British forces before them.

The Greeks, meanwhile, had been overwhelmed. The last of their forces, in the west, capitulated on 21st April, leaving the British to confront the Germans alone. There was a last stand at Thermopylae, but the German assaults proved too strong. Australian and New Zealand troops managed to hold the perimeter while the British organised an evacuation to the island of Crete.

Within a day, the Germans had come after them. On 20th May, the skies over Crete suddenly filled with German aircraft and a relentless bombing raid followed. Eyewitnesses reported that the Luftwaffe came from every direction in successive waves. Often, there were more than sixty planes at a time, and they were flying in such close formation that the sky went dark.

The Germans had the sky to themselves. There was no air cover by the Royal Air Force.

The Luftwaffe was carrying men as well as bombs. The Seventh German Fleigerdivision parachuted down, together with an entire field hospital, doctors, orderlies, bed and Red Cross flags. It was the first major airbourne assault in military history. The local Cretan population were waiting for the Germans, and killed every parachutist they could found. The slaughter was such that the Fleigerdivision lost around half its strength. Several of the Germans were dead before they reached the ground.

German control of the air greatly hampered the soldiers on the ground, but had no effect on their will to resist. A Maori sergeant with the New Zealand contingent on Crete later told what it was like.

'We were unable to move owing to the unremitting bombing and machine gunning from the German dive-bombers, but when the Sun went down, we were able to fight back. We fixed our bayonets and immediately it was dark, we charged, yelling the Haka, our war-cry. Our first obstacle was a solid line of German machine guns, but we quickly overran then and after a great fight lasting until dawn, we killed practically every German who was there. But then, when daylight returned, waves of German airbourne reinforcements began to arrive. Within a few hours, around one hundred and thirty Nazi troop-carriers, escorted by clouds of fighters, had landed and throughout the day, we were attacked by more than two hundred dive-bombers. We sheathed our bayonets and lay hidden in the rocks or in the drains. With the welcome cloak of darkness, we fixed our bayonets and charged and again cut the enemy to pieces. This went on for four days and four nights.'

The parachutists were also coming down in the mountains, and so many of

Original caption: Ground mechanic with ammunition belt.

them were killed by Greek soldiers that 'in the battle area, it was impossible to walk more than three yards without stepping over dead Germans.'

The balance of the struggle for Crete nevertheless inexorably set against the British and they had to be evacuated from the island. About 45,000 had left by the time the campaign came to an end on 27th May. Some 9,000 became prisoners, according to German estimates, and 6,000 were reported either killed or missing. Hitler could now be satisfied at last that he cleared the ground for his projected invasion of Russia. He looked forward to another blitzkrieg victory, but in this he was severely mistaken.

The triumph of blitzkrieg, in Poland, western Europe and the Balkans, had been influenced by the confines of the battlegrounds and the brevity of the campaigns. No battlefront so far assaulted by the German lightning war had been wider than 300 miles and no campaign had lasted more than around two months. The great maw of Russia, where the front was to be six times as wide and space to manoeuvrer or make strategic withdrawals was virtually infinite, was quite another matter.

Heinz Guderian was appalled at the prospect. Guderian was acutely aware that the main guiding principle of blitzkrieg, the concentration of maximum force against a single objective, was going to be undermined, if not completely dissipated. As the German forces advanced into Russia, they would diverge further and further away from one another instead of drawing closer and becoming more concentrated. This would dissipate the power of their attacks and made the quick disorientating punch of blitzkrieg redundant. The nature of the ground in Russia removed the vital asset of mobility and the apparently endless reserves at the disposal of the Red Army meant that they could recoup losses rapidly. None of these adverse conditions had obtained during the halcyon days of blitzkrieg success in 1940 and early 1941.

Almost the only blitzkrieg element left for the Russian campaign was surprise, as Ernst Preuss observed on invasion day.

'We advanced at the beginning, on the first day of the war, on the 22nd June 1941, when we marched into Russia. It was the longest day of my life. It started at 0500 hours. We had been told that the Russians had attacked us. so off we marched to teach them a lesson. We had no enemy contact, we just advanced and advanced, with the tanks, and that continued into the night with hardly a pause and it wasn't until the next day that we met the first light resistance.'

Hans Lehmann encountered Russians rather sooner than Preuss but he had no doubt that the invasion was unexpected.

'We were stationed on the border, everywhere in the woods and so on. And then it began abruptly, into Russia we went. The Russians were stationed close to the border on the other side, and they were caught totally by surprise.'

Luftwaffe paratrooper armed with machine pistol and hand grenade.

Fw-200 Condor bomber and crew shortly before take-off.

A squadron of Fw-200 Condor bombers shortly before take-off.

THE LUFTWAFFE:
EAGLES ASCENDING 1939-1942

The creation of the Luftwaffe which, like the Greek goddess Athena from the forehead of Zeus, sprang fully armed into view in 1936, had been part of Hitler's policy of re arming Germany in secret. One of the many punitive provisions of the Treaty of Versailles of 1919, which ended the First World War, had been a ban on a German air force as well as substantial reductions in the size of the German army and navy. Clandestine rearmament took place nevertheless, and Hitler announced it to a shocked world in 1935.

Karl Born remembers how the existence of the new air force was revealed.

'There was an air show in London, and Hitler disguised his men, the NS flying corps, so that they could take part. He wanted to see if the English would object, but when they made no objections, then they were told 'This is the German Luftwaffe!'

The build up of the Luftwaffe had been concealed behind an apparently innocent interest in gliding and flying clubs. The manufacture of warplanes had been masked by Lufthansa, the German civil airline, which flew passengers in Junkers, Fokker, Messerschmitt and other aircraft that were designed for easy conversion to military use.

The Hitler Youth, the Hitlerjugend, had been at the core of the policy of rearming Germany while at the same deceiving her erstwhile enemies. Outwardly, the Hitler Youth catered for boyish enthusiasms and a sense of adventure. What was really happening was the creation of the most highly trained, highly motivated and most militarised teenagers in the world. The future pilots of the Second World War joined the Flieger-Hitlerjugend and began their training building and flying model gliders in order to learn the principles of flight. Afterwards, they graduated to a gliding test which involved being shot into the air attached to a simple glider wing. They used this to fly a short distance, and then come safely in to land. Eventually, the Flieger-Hitlerjugend graduated to flying gliders and piston-engined aircraft, all ostensibly in the name of boyish fun.

The degree of enthusiasm invoked in the 'flying' Hitler Youth was exampled by Alfred Wagner who was so keen to fly for the Fatherland that, during the Second World War, he volunteered for duty on every possible occasion.

'When you're young, enthusiasm takes you over. It's like a driving force you can't control. I volunteered for the Luftwaffe when I was 17. To me, it was a marvellous adventure. Flying was enormous fun, and I was full of enthusiasm for it, if we were asked to volunteer to fly somewhere, I was always first in the queue!'

The heroes young men like Alfred Wagner longed to emulate were the intrepid aces of the First World War whose daring in dog-fights with the enemy had made them into legends - Baron von Richthofen, the 'Red Baron', Verner Voss, Max von Muller, Ernst Udet and Hermann Goering, who later became head of the Luftwaffe.

Goering, who first met Adolf Hitler in 1922 and became a keen disciple, was the son of a diplomat. He made a distinguished name for himself in the First World War and became famous as one of Germany's top air aces, with twenty 'kills' to his credit. At age twenty-five, after the 'Red Baron's' death in action in 1918, Goering succeeded him as commander of the renowned Richthofen Squadron. Goering was commander for only four months before Germany's defeat and surrender and his great personal vanity as well as his strong sense of nationalism were mightily offended by the terms of the Versailles treaty. Like many Germans, Goering felt the armed forces had been dishonoured and after falling under the extraordinary spell Hitler exerted over his followers, he joined the Nazi Party determined to right this wrong.

From Hitler's point of view, Goering's personal devotion and his exploits in the First World War fitted him perfectly to head the new Luftwaffe he intended to forge. With Ernst Rohm, another veteran of the War and chief of the SA, the Nazi stormtroopers, Goering became a principle lieutenant of the future Führer.

Although Goering was awed by Hitler's personality and often acted like his minion, he had a charisma of his own which could fuel enthusiasm in others. One of those he personally inspired was Hajo Hermann, who later flew 370 missions with the Luftwaffe and downed ten Allied aircraft.

'Goering actually determined my career as a flier. I was an infantryman and scrabbling around with a steel helmet and machine gun on the army training ground near Berlin. He rode up, wearing the uniform of an infantry general, and called down to me, 'Well, what's it like down there, then? Isn't it a bit tough? Wouldn't you rather come up here to me?' and he pointed upwards towards the sky.

'At the time, I had no idea who he was. We didn't have television, so we weren't familiar with the high-ups in the armed forces. But he pointed to the sky and said: 'Up there, become an airman.' And I said, 'Yes indeed, Herr General!' Shortly afterwards I was ordered to go to Berlin for an air force medical examination and then it began.'

Later, during the War, Hajo Hermann received special favour from Goering after he had developed the night-fighter technique known as the 'Wild Boar'. This was an attempt to put a stop to the night bombing of Berlin by the Royal Air Force in 1943 and 1944, and involved the use of Messerschmitt 109s as nightfighters. Guided only by ground radio, the Me-109s successfully hunted down the RAF bombers. Hajo Hermann refined his 'Wild Boar' with camouflage: the undersides of the aircraft were painted black and an additional flame dampener was added over the exhaust stubs. Some of the Me-109s were equipped with a whistle device that helped the ground crews identify the Luftwaffe aircraft as they returned from their missions.

The 'Wild Boar' and its successes came to Goering's attention and Hajo Hermann found himself shooting up the ranks.

'Goering promoted me immediately, that happened quite rapidly. At the beginning of 1944, I was a captain and at the end of the year I was a colonel. He put me up for a higher decoration, which I was then awarded by Hitler.'

Hitler followed Goering's recommendation even though, at that stage in the War, he was out of favour with the Führer. Hitler's disillusionment dated from 1940, when, despite Goering's swaggering and boasting about 'his' Luftwaffe, they had lost the Battle of Britain and therefore ruined the chances for another successful German invasion.

Hajo Hermann acknowledges that Goering made mistakes but this had no effect on his loyalty.

'I cannot with the best will in the world make a disparaging judgment about this man because he did too many good things for me. He gave me his trust and raised me to higher positions. I don't bear an absolute admiration for him, but as Shakespeare said, 'Taken all in all, he was a man,'

In 1936, Hajo Hermann flew with the Luftwaffe's Condor Legion in Spain, where they supported the Nationalist forces of General Francisco Franco and gave an awesome demonstration of what Europe could expect from a future war. The seeds of the Spanish Civil War, which began on 18 July 1936, had been sown five years earlier, when the rise to power of republican liberals had forced the King, Alfonso XIII, into exile. Franco, who proved to be a dictator in the Hitler-Mussolini mould, rebelled against the anti-militarist policies of the liberal government and invaded Spain from Spanish Morocco. In Germany, Hitler's sympathies were naturally with Franco and the Condor Legion was detailed for 'special duty' in Spain.

The Legion consisted of four bombers squadrons, forty-eight aircraft in all, and four fighter squadrons backed by anti-aircraft and anti-tank units. With this, the curtain went up on a new and terrifying form of air warfare: the blitzkrieg, with its heavy bombing raids and dive-bombing tactics, as demonstrated by the Ju-87 'Stuka'. The First World War in the air had been a

THE AIRCRAFT IN RETROSPECT: HE-111

The He-111 was the most common bomber in service with the Luftwaffe. Although it was officially designated as a medium bomber this twin-engine machine was in fact the heaviest bomber, which was widely available to the Luftwaffe. Although this aircraft was never as common as the more successful Ju-88 it achieved much more fame. Designed by Siegfried and Walter Günter in the early 1930s it was often described as the "Wolf in sheep's clothing", as in the pre-war era it masqueraded as a transport aircraft in order to avoid the restrictions of the Treaty of Versailles.

The He-111 is perhaps the most famous symbol of the German bomber force (Kampfwaffe) due its distinctive leaf like wing shape and "Greenhouse" nose, which gave excellent all round observation. The Heinkel 111 was the only medium/heavy Luftwaffe bomber during the early stages of the Second World War. lt proved reliable and efficient in all the early campaigns suffering only modest losses until the Battle of Britain, when its weak defensive armament exposed its vulnerability. As a combat aircraft the He-111 proved capable of sustaining heavy damage and remaining airborne. As the war progressed the He-111 was used in an ever increasing variety of roles on every front throughout the war and in every conceivable role. The He-111 saw service as a strategic bomber during the Battles for Poland, Norway, Holland and France. lt was heavily involved in the Battle of Britain, but also saw service as a torpedo bomber in the Battle of the Atlantic, a medium bomber and a transport aircraft on the Western Front, the Eastern Front and the North African Fronts. Later in the war, with the German bomber force redundant, the He-111 was converted to use as a transport aircraft and downgraded to a logistics role. Despite being constantly upgraded it became obsolete during the latter part of the war, but the failure of the Luftwaffe to design and produce a worthy successor meant the He-111 continued to be produced until 1944. Some 5600 of all variants were produced.

relatively gentlemanly business, with pilots jousting in dog-fights like medieval knights in the lists and adopting a chivalrous approach to their opponents. By 1936, all that had disappeared. The Condor Legion in Spain was out to terrorise, annihilate and paralyse the republican forces and on 27th April 1937 was accused of atrocity over the bombing of Guernica, the cultural and spiritual home of the Basques.

It was market day, and Guernica was crowded with visitors from the environs round about. Suddenly, it was later reported, the sky filled with Heinkel 111s and Junkers-52s, escorted by fighters, and the crowds in the town square were pounded with high explosives and strafed with machine-gun fire. Incendiary bombs rained down, setting fire to buildings. The Mayor of Guernica later told newspaper reporters: 'They bombed and bombed and bombed.'

One reporter arrived in Guernica soon after the aircraft departed:

'On both sides of the road, men, women and children were sitting, dazed. I saw a priest and stopped the car and went up to him. His face was blackened, his clothes in tatters. He couldn't talk and pointed to the flames about four miles away, then whispered: 'Aviones...bombas...much, mucho...'

Smoke, flames, the nauseating smell of burning human flesh and the dust and grit from collapsed buildings filled the air.

'It was impossible to go down many of the streets, because they were walls of flame. Debris was piled high. The shocked survivors all had the same story to tell: aeroplanes, bullets, bombs, fire.'

Despite such dramatic reports, the bombing of Guernica became controversial when the Condor Legion denied involvement, even though the town contained military installations - a communications centre and a munitions factory - that could have counted as legitimate targets. Blame was ascribed instead to the Nationalists, who, it was said, had destroyed Guernica themselves. Experts called in to examine the ruins confirmed that the pattern of destruction evidenced explosions from the ground rather than from the air. However, the style and power of the attack on Guernica, as described, bore a chilling resemblance to the way the Luftwaffe later fought in the blitzkrieg campaigns against Poland and in western Europe. Then, it became clear, the destruction of Guernica, as reported, had been only a rehearsal.

Hajo Hermann found that the Condor Legion did not always have things their own way. The Republicans, too, were receiving aid from the outside. On receiving suitable payment in gold, the Russians sent them their best fighter, the Polikarpov 1-16 Rata. The Rata was the first in the world to combine cantilever monoplane wings with retractable landing gear at a time when almost all fighters were biplanes.

Hajo Hermann remembers what happened when the Luftwaffe aircraft had to confront the Rata, an aircraft the German pilots came to respect, with good reason.

'The Polikarpov 1-16 Rata was the best plane that turned up in Spain. On one occasion, I was shot at by a Rata. It flew in an arc from in front of me, flying past and the rear gun was fired directly into the cockpit. Afterwards, there were quite a lot of bullet holes in my plane. Some of my comrades in the Condor Legion got as many as 250 bullets in battles with the Rata.

'They were really hard planes to fight against. You couldn't see them against the horizon. They used to come from Alcala de Henares, Getafe, the areas around Madrid and climbed up rapidly and you couldn't really see them over that area. Then, suddenly there they were!

'You couldn't hear the Rata, either. That was the peculiar thing.

In the air, everything takes place absolutely silently, secretively, and then suddenly, from out of the silence, comes death. That's what it was like. You thought you were watching the Ratas from a distance, then a tiny spot suddenly becomes enormous, with a huge engine in front of your nose, and they're firing at you.

'The Ratas often approached our planes head on. That was dangerous for us. We could defend ourselves very well from the rear. We had a rear gunner and down below in the bowl, in the 'pot' as we called it, we had an observer who could fire to the rear. We also had machine guns pointing out of the side windows but we were vulnerable in the front. That was why an officer on the General Staff, Kraft von Delmensingen, ordered machine guns to be fitted to our wings.'

The deadly nature of the Rata was made clear when Hajo Hermann was flying a JU-52 to attack a Republican position at Bilbao, in northern Spain.

'Another of the Condor pilots flew in front of me to the left. Suddenly, the Rata flew between us and our man was a goner. His aircraft began to burn and immediately turned into a fiery, red ball. The plane just disintegrated and fell to Earth flaking into pieces.

'It was a tremendous shock, but only for a tenth of a second or so, and it taught me a lesson for the future. When you're flying in war, you have to keep on towards the target. That's your duty and you must do it.

'Of course, you know you can suffer the same fate - that's the way war is. But it's no good dwelling on it, even when you've just seen a comrade blown out of the sky. It always seemed to me to be so futile to expend a lot of emotion on the victim. Later, I went to war having made the decision once and for all, to engage in war, do it well, do it with determination. You have to reach your targets and you have to win.'

In the assembly shop, leads and cables are still being laid and connected. Another Ju-87 dive bomber can soon leave the works tended by the skilled hands of capable experts.

Hajo Hermann had had other plans for his Luftwaffe career when he was sent to Spain. An unfriendly commander, he believes, was responsible.

'I went to Spain, I think, because my commander in Thuringen wanted to get rid of me. I had done something undisciplined for an airman, and when this commander was told to send one man from our group to Spain, he chose me. 'At first I regarded it as a punishment and I was dismayed because I had other aims. I was just about to go on a 'blind-flying' course in order to train as a 'blind-flying' tutor but he said 'Listen you can do that later, go to Spain first. Sign this paper stating that you will keep everything we talk about a secret, because officially, the government isn't supposed to know anything about sending German airman to Spain. Off you go, then, you will be there for three weeks and are to fly Nationalist troops from Morocco over the Straits of Gibraltar to Spain. General Franco is waiting there for them'.

'After a while in Spain, I changed my mind and instead of a punishment, it began to look like an adventure. I travelled to Cadiz on a steam boat together with several others from another garrison and in Cadiz we had our first experience of war. A very simple double-decker plane approached, a French plane and dropped a few small bombs. It didn't look like much of an attack, but the bombs exploded smack against the hull of our ship. A little later, a Spanish battle ship sailed up and fired shells across the harbour so that fountains of water spouted up all round us. I used to like the pictures of the sea battles in the First World War, Skagerrak and so on where water fountains spouted up, but I had never experienced it and here I saw it for the first time. That's how the Spanish episode began.

'When I arrived in Toledo, it was in October 1936, there had been a lot of fighting and it looked pretty grim. I saw the corpses and awful scenes where the Republicans had killed priests and nuns. They lay everywhere on the ground, blood everywhere, in the villages too.

'Later, we flew from Salamanca to attack Madrid, where the Republicans had ensconced themselves in the university district. Madrid was a very heavily defended town. But we didn't spread terror there, like some people say, or drop bombs down into the middle of the city. Our task was to bomb the front line positions.

'We also attacked the northern front line. But it was all very primitive down there in Spain. The Spaniards were totally unprepared for fighting on their own territory, as I discovered after we were ordered to fly from Burgos to attack the front line in the north. Most of the harbours in the north, like Bilbao or Oviedo, had been occupied by the Republicans. It was an important industrial area, with iron ore and coal deposits. I was given the task of flying in advance to Burgos to prepare the airfield for missions and it turned out to be very, very difficult.

There was nothing there. I had hardly any materials and so I spoke to the Archbishop of Bilbao and said that I needed the floodlights he had at his cathedral to use on the airfield. He didn't like that at all. He refused at first, but then I told him: 'We are fighting against atheists, you must surely agree with that'. Well, that changed his mind and I got my floodlights.'

Service with the Condor Legion in the Spanish Civil War afforded Hajo Hermann a great deal of varied experience in air warfare.

'I flew transport missions, carried over two thousand troops across the sea, and was then re-equipped for bombing. I carried six 250 kg bombs in the JU 52 and flew different missions, mostly against ships, mainly against Mexican and Soviet supply ships that sailed into the harbour at Cartagena with supplies for the Republicans.

'When we flew on missions, we were escorted by the Italian Savoya Marchetti 81. I think it was called, and the C 32. They were quite ingenious machines, equally good as our Heinkel- 51 fighters.

'There were substantial air battles during attacks on the suburbs of Madrid which the Republicans defended bitterly, the university quarter. We were busy dropping our bombs and our Heinkels suffered considerable losses'

Hermann used his opportunities in Spain to experiment with new ways of fighting from air. He flew out one day and dropped stones and iron bars into the Straits of Gibraltar.

'That was an invention of mine. It was considered quite mad, of course, but it wasn't a bad idea at all. When we flew over the Straits - we were heavily loaded with armed men - the Russian destroyers used to fire up at us. We were hit too, in the front and the rear. Many of our passengers were badly injured. They made a terrible fuss. You'd think the world was coming to an end.

'So I told them: 'Now we'll send our greetings to the people down below' and got together some bars and old junk which I'd loaded up into the rear of the plane close by the door, where the commander of this unit sat. I said to him that when he got the signal he should open the door a little and push all the junk out with his foot, that would make some lovely noises down below and it did too. The noise caused by non-dynamic objects like that is enormous. I know because I once experience it myself. A toolbox fell out of a plane by accident and landed on the ground with a tremendous crash, it was indescribable. So I did it on purpose this time, and though we didn't hit much, there was plenty of noise and people on the ground were terrified.'

If Hermann had been sent to Spain in the first place because of indiscipline, his behaviour did not improve that much once he was there.

'General Mola was Nationalist Commander in Chief of the northern front line in Spain and I had to report to him to apologise for being rude about the

Clouds, waves, and far-flung wide open spaces - there the seaplane pilots hold away.

The fighter pilot at the front airdrome is attentively following the return of his comrades who have just paid one of their numerous visits to Tommy Atkins in his island home.

Spaniards. I had complained that they worked too slowly, and I was to apologise, but before I even had time to open my mouth to excuse myself, General Mola said, in French which I myself spoke: ' Listen, why have you given me so few flak guns?' At the time I was involved in training the Spanish soldiers to use flak, so I assured General Mola that more of the guns would be coming and he seemed satisfied with that. He seemed to forget all about my rude remarks. I was supposed to be sent home in disgrace, but instead, I was allowed to stay in Spain.

'After that, I was on a mission, flying from Melilla in Morocco to attack Cartagena, but there was a problem. Italy, Germany, Britain and France had agreed to patrol the coasts of Spain so that neither the Nationalists nor the Republicans could bring in new forces. At least that's what we, the Germans, said we were there for and the others, I suppose, would have done their best to turn back my aircraft. Fortunately, Admiral Fischl was with his fleet, anchored outside the three-mile limit by the Costa del Sol, near Almeria and Cartagena. He ordered a floodlight to be switched on so that I could see my way to Cartagena. That was his idea of non-intervention!'.

The Spanish Civil War ended with a Nationalist victory on 28th March 1939, when General Franco marched into Madrid. The Condor Legion departed for home just as events were prefiguring the outbreak of the Second World War less than six months later. Two weeks before the civil war in Spain came to an end, the forces of Nazi Germany had occupied Czechoslovakia, contrary to the agreement made with Hitler by Neville Chamberlain and Edouard Daladier, the prime ministers of Britain and France, at the time of the Munich Crisis late in 1938. This latest aggression on the part of the Third Reich was followed by another, the invasion of Poland on 1 September 1939 and this time, Britain and France did not stand by and watch, but declared war.

The campaign in Poland, which barely outlasted September, was the first illustration of what the Luftwaffe could do in a full-scale, all-out war. At the time of Munich, the Luftwaffe had already been a mighty force, with 1,669 aircraft, including 453 fighters, 582 bombers and 159 dive-bombers. By the eve of the War only nine months later, it had more than doubled its size, with 3,7500 aircraft, of which 1,170 were bombers, 335 were dive-bombers and 1,125 were fighters, mainly Me-109s, and 195 twin-engined fighters, mostly Me-110s. Energetic aircraft production ensured that these numbers grew as the War progressed, particularly after the brilliant Albert Speer assumed responsibility. No other European power had an air force as large or as impressive as this, nor did any have experience comparable to the 'rehearsal' by the Condor Legion in Spain.

The value of that experience was clear during the prelude to the invasion of

Poland, when the Luftwaffe bombed, strafed and destroyed virtually at will and while not entirely destroying the Polish Air Force as had been planned, rendered it more or less useless. The Poles had only around 500 aircraft, compared to 1,600 Luftwaffe planes, but it was not simply a question of numbers. The Polish planes were primitive compared to their state-of-the-art opponents and the shock surprise of blitzkrieg attack caught the Polish armed forces critically off balance.

Hajo Hermann was there in the opening moments of the Polish campaign.

'Surveying the army advancing from the air, It looked just overwhelming.

Wherever we were advancing, over an area of around 200 kms., you could see where the guns were firing or the houses were burning and the fighting was taking place. The whole landscape seemed to be consumed by war. But I thought about the way the Poles had betrayed us after the First World War and I said to myself: 'Well now you are taking part, this is your chance to erase the great injustice the Poles have done us.'

By 1940, other landscapes 'consumed by war', blitzkrieg war, enabled the German armed forces to conquer Norway, Denmark, the Low Countries and France, all in quick, unstoppable succession. Norway, together with Denmark, was invaded on 9th April. Oslo was heavily bombed by the Luftwaffe and a British newspaper corresponded was there to record the result.

'With German bombers wheeling overhead like birds of prey, the rattle of machine gun fire on the outskirts of Oslo and the heavy thud of bombs echoing down the fjord, the bewildered crowds in the city's streets were sheltering in doorways and flattening themselves against the walls. With a piercing crescendo of noise, a great four-engined machine dived right over the housetops and streaked skywards again, its tail gun covering the length of the street.

'The Germans had landed at Moss, twenty miles from Oslo on the east side of the fjord. Their ships were in the fjord and their aircraft had bombed the airport. German bombers were wheeling over a ridge at Fetsund, also twenty miles from Oslo. Black puffs of anti-aircraft fire pitted the sky for the whole length of the ridge. The thud of bombs, the rattle of machine guns echoed in the air. The Luftwaffe's target was Kjeller, the Norwegian military air base.'

Norway was conquered and occupied. So was Denmark, but the one flaw in the run of German success in western Europe in the early summer of 1940 was the escape of the British Expeditionary Force together with large numbers of French and Belgian soldiers, from the beaches of Dunkirk in northern France. Hermann Goering believed that these men, vulnerable and exposed as they waited for rescue from England, could be easily finished off by the Luftwaffe. He was wrong. In a foretaste of what they would encounter in the Battle of

Britain, the Luftwaffe was fended off by the Royal Air Force in a series of punishing, hard-fought battles. Hajo Hermann was flying over the Dunkirk area while the Royal Navy and the fleet of private 'little ships' were lifting the soldiers off the beaches and piers and the RAF was on guard.

'We found ourselves on our own over the harbour at Dunkirk. It was teeming with British soldiers down below and I attempted to unload my bombs onto two of the ships. I missed, and the Hurricanes came after us, blazing gunfire. Our plane was hit and smoke began pouring out of one of the engines. The other engine packed up. The plane slid down into the water about one hundred metres from the beach. The entire cockpit was smashed up. 'Suddenly, we were under the water. But thank goodness, we all got out. I had a hand injury, but I had to ignore that. What was more important was that the escaping English weren't too far away. So we crawled cautiously onto the beach, through the surf, always crawling, always to the east, away from the English. So, we were saved. But for us, the operation at Dunkirk was over.'

The Luftwaffe destroyed the town and the harbour at Dunkirk, setting them alight with incendiary bombs. But they were unable to make good Goering's boast that they could annihilate the men on the beaches. A total of 338,000 escaped back to England, to fight another day. It was a day that would soon arrive.

By 22nd June 1940, when France capitulated and Britain became the only combatant still free to oppose the Nazis, it seemed only a matter of time before the island country was invaded and added to Hitler's new European empire. Despite the failure at Dunkirk, Hermann Goering, in his flamboyant buccaneering fashion, was certain that his Luftwaffe was on the brink of another spectacular victory.

There were several reasons why he was mistaken. Firstly, the R.A.F. was the first up-to-date air force the Luftwaffe had encountered. On the brink of the Battle of Britain in mid-1940, statistics appeared to prove that the Royal Air Force had scant chances, with only 1,911 first-line aircraft compared to the Germans' 4,161. Three Luftflotten, numbers 2,3 and 5 were deployed on airfields stretching from Brittany to Norway, including 898 bombers, 708 single-engined and 202 twin-engined fighters. Lutflotte 2, based in northeastern France, Belgium, the Netherlands and northern Germany was to attack the southeast of England. The western half of England was the responsibility of Luftflotte 3, which used airfields sited from the French Atlantic coast to west of the River Seine. Luftflotte 5, based in Norway and Denmark was to make diversionary attacks on targets in northern Britain.

These forces, though formidable, suffered from several disadvantages.

The first was that it was being required to act out of character. The

Luftwaffe had been designed as 'flying artillery' acting in support of ground forces, not for a strategic bombing campaign or for a prolonged air war.

Until the Battle of Britain began in mid-August 1940, Germany's pilots had not yet faced a well-armed, well-equipped, up to date air force. They had enjoyed a comparatively easy run, operating in attack areas close to Germany against inferior enemies, and operating over land. Britain, too, was not that far from the Germans' reach after the conquests of 1940, a minimum of only twenty one miles across the English Channel. The Channel, however, was an important deciding factor, as it had always been when the defence of Britain was at stake. So was the presence there of the Royal Navy. That made it potentially hostile territory for Luftwaffe aircraft flying over it, whether it was to tangle with the RAF or to 'blitz' British cities.

Although they appeared well placed, on the coasts of Europe nearest to Britain, the range of the Luftwaffe aircraft was limited by this narrow, but deceptive waterway. The Me-109, for instance, had a radius of action, out and home, of little more than 100 miles , with only around 80 minutes of tactical flying time. This was barely enough to reach London and do damage before having to fly home and, hopefully, avoid ditching in the Channel.

The rapid conquest of western Europe had been exhilarating for the Germans, but the very speed of it presented new and taxing problems. There was no time before the attack on Britain to prepare new air bases and set up adequate supply lines. There were no local facilities for the repair of damaged aircraft, which had to be taken back to Germany instead. There was also a critical lack of reserves, no reliable method of plotting the positions of RAF aircraft and no ground-to-air facilities for guiding the Luftwaffe planes.

The new difficulties the Luftwaffe encountered in the Battle of Britain were largely due to Hermann Goering's lack of foresight, his poor planning and overweening confidence in the might of 'his' Luftwaffe. These faults at the top were compounded by the fact that many Luftwaffe aircraft were too poorly armed to be certain of a safe flight across the Channel without a fighter escort. Hajo Hermann remembers how hamstrung he felt when he flew over London.

'I bombed London, because the English were already at work bombing Berlin and very heavily. And we only did it, by way of retaliation. We hit back, and Adolf Hitler, the evil man, always used to say, if the British stop, then we will stop too. But the British didn't stop. So God help me, I flew to London twenty-three times and dropped my bombs down onto it. There was no precise targeting, no strategic purpose in what I did. I felt bad about that. In the city and I don't know what other parts of the town, it was very regrettable.'

Unteroffizier Peter Stahl, pilot of a Junkers 88 had similar misgivings when engaged in bombing London in October 1940.

'During our approach flight to London, it becomes almost spooky in our glazed housing. The searchlights have lit up the clouds, so we are flying blind and feel as if we are hanging in our fuzzy surroundings, sitting inside a white cotton-wool ball with no idea what is happening above and below us. I had to concentrate really hard to 'pull together my whole brain' as we used to say, to avoid making errors. That takes nerve! My only wish was to be out of here and quick.'

The blitz on London began on 7th September 1940, with a raid on the capital during the evening and the East End suffering most of the damage.

The description of the raid by a 16-year old eyewitness living in the London docklands was typical of the capital's first experience of being directly under German fire.

'The air raid siren went at quarter to five in the afternoon. We heard gunfire and the sound of aircraft, so we all went into our Anderson shelter. The planes came over in three batches, we could hear them very clearly, and the guns sent up a terrific barrage. We could hear bombs whistling down all round as we cowered in the back of the shelter, expecting to be hit at any moment.

'Bombs were dropping in a field behind us, and we thought that if they didn't hit us, they would surely hit our house. Our shelter shook and so did we. We ate sweets and tried not to mind. All the time, fire engines were rushing past clanging their bells.

'When the All Clear sounded and we started to come out of the shelter, my brother said: 'Hasn't it got dark?' It was a great smoke cloud all over the sky, thick, black smoke which made our faces dirty, just standing there. We thought for a moment that our house was on fire, but it was red from the reflection of burning buildings round about. We could see at least half a dozen fires blazing and great flames shooting up into the sky.

The cloud of smoke rising over the East End of London could be seen miles away. Another eyewitness saw it from far out in the countryside.

'I was driving back from Oxford with friends early in the evening and we were still miles out in the country when we saw a huge column of smoke hanging far away over the house tops. At first we didn't know whether it was merely a cloud. But we guessed what it was when we came on the dramatic spectacle of street after street lined with people, every head turned upward and eastwards. I reach home in London to find a bomb had dropped in the next street. I was trying to investigate this when I got a call to go to the scene of the fire. A general's daughter, a girl of 19, an ambulance driver, begged to come with me.

'We were waiting for the bus when the air raid warning sounded again. We

The Ju-52 was the workhorse of the Luftwaffe for logistics transport and logistics missions. The aircraft was easy to maintain and carried a reasonable payload. It could take great punishment, which was fortunate, as the machine was sluggish and in consequence was easy prey for enemy fighters. First introduced into service in 1931, over 5000 of these rugged machines saw service with the Luftwaffe in every theatre of war.

knew at once where the fire was, because this line of buses immediately came to a halt. They were held up at the other end. We walked some distance. There were heavy bursts of gunfire and we put on our tin hats. A taxi drew up in the middle of the road. 'Will you take me to the fire?' I asked. 'I'll get you as near to it as I possible can' said the driver. Then began a mad ride through London.

'In one street, about a dozen firemen, with hoses and fire-pumps, had just managed to extinguish one fire. They told us factories had been hit. It wasn't too easy to breathe. Above the glare, we could see the curtain of smoke and above that two balloons.

'Suddenly, we heard a whirring, rushing sound. 'That's a bomb' someone shouted. 'Fall flat!' We flung ourselves in the gutter, in a sort of human chain. A few moments passed. Afterwards, we took shelter in a garage. When the activity overhead died down, we came out again. What we had seen before was nothing to what we saw now.

'The whole air was a bright blaze of gold, with those two balloons still floating above. We shouted for our taxi man. When he arrived, he said he had been blown to the ground by a bomb. Just as we started off again in the taxi, we heard first a rushing, then a heavy explosion and a brilliant firework display in the road directly in our path. A bomb had blocked the road.

'Later, I talked with a woman who drove in a car over London Bridge and back over Tower Bridge during the evening. She said that nothing moved her so much as the sight of the Tower of London. 'It stood there squat and solid and contemptuous, with the whole sky on fire behind it,' she said. 'It symbolised the whole of our history. It will take a good deal more than Hitler to shake us.'

Defiant attitudes like this were bad news for Hermann Goering. He had assumed that the British could be terrorised into submission by bombing and strafing. Gripped by this delusion, he had made a serious blunder in sending his Luftwaffe to attack Britain's cities while neglecting to press home the offensive against the British Fighter Command.

Goering's blunders multiplied when he dispatched bombers to assault cities as far apart as Swansea, Aberdeen and Belfast. On one raid, attempting to safeguard the dispersed bomber streams, the Luftwaffe lost twenty-four fighters to the RAF's fourteen. The effect of the Luftwaffe offensive was also blunted by poor intelligence gathering. The wrong airfields and factories were targeted.

As the Battle of Britain progressed, the loss of RAF fighters was heavy, but the loss to the Luftwaffe was heavier. On 15th July, fifty German aircraft were destroyed in one day. Between 13th and 18th August, three hundred and fifty German aircraft were lost. The RAF lost one hundred and seventy.

In Britain, the summer of 1940 was bright, sunny and warm, the perfect flying weather, and thousands of people in the south east and along the coast had perfect visibility as they watched Spitfires and Me-109s jousting high above in the bright blue summer sky. Luftwaffe bombers could be clearly seen as they flew over in packed formations. One eyewitness watched Spitfires attacking a fleet of Luftwaffe bombers over Surrey.

'The whole panorama of the beautiful Surrey countryside was laid out before us, but soon the German bombers could be heard high up above. Our Anti-aircraft batteries opened fire immediately and the sky seemed full of fighter aircraft going up in pursuit. A German bombers suddenly hurtled out of the sky like a falling leaf. The pilot managed to regain some control as he near the earth and it seemed as if a safe landing might have been possible, but he made a sudden dive, hitting the ground. The machine immediately burst into an inferno of flame and smoke. It was a terrible scene, taking place just down below us in the valley in brilliant sunshine.

'Meanwhile, the RAF fighters were zooming in all directions and we could hear the rattle of machine gun fire above us. A big black German bombers planed right across our vision about three hundred feet from the ground, with engines off, obviously trying to land. Then came a burst of machine gun fire as he scraped over the roof of a farmhouse nearby. it was astonishing to us that the occupants of the bomber in such a perilous position could still think of machine-gunning the farmhouse as they passed over the roof and pancaked into a field half a mile further on, apparently undamaged.

'While this was going on, anti-aircraft batteries were sending up shells at a terrific rate. Shells were bursting in the wood behind us and we felt that any moment, some splinters might descend upon us. After a short interval, we saw a formation of Spitfires bring down two more bombers on the distant hills.

'The next thing we saw, a group of German bombers, hotly pursued by Spitfires, were seen making for the coast. The action had lasted thirty-five minutes. When it was over, the Surrey countryside was peaceful once again and the only evidence of the battle were the smoking ruins of the German bombers in the fields below us.'

The rate of loss suffered by the Luftwaffe in engagements like this was a particular nightmare for Ernst Udet, whose friend, Hermann Goering, had appointed him chief of Luftwaffe supply and procurement and head of its technical office. Udet may have been an ace pilot in the First World War, but he was no organiser. He made a complete mess of the flow of new aircraft required to replace the Luftwaffe's losses. When Goering found out, his first thought was to hide the truth in order to protect his friend, but Udet had another solution. Ostensibly, he was killed in an aircraft crash, but in fact committed suicide.

The shortcomings of the German aircraft, especially the Messerschmitt 110 were also exposed during the Battle of Britain. Later in the War, after 1942, Anton Heinemann was a less-than-satisfied Me-110 pilot.

'The Me-110 had six guns facing forwards, but because the plane couldn't fly for too long, they were retired. We were given the Junkers-88, which a large additional tank, so that we had a larger margin of safety if we encountered fog or had to be diverted to another airfield.'

The Me-109, whose dogfights with the Spitfire gave it a gladiatorial image, had a different Achilles Heel, but a no less serious one. It consumed aviation fuel at a great rate, so much so that by the time it had reached the war zone over southern England, it had only about half an hour of combat time left.

Luftwaffe pilots were at a disadvantage here. If they were shot down or had to parachute to safety, they found themselves in enemy territory, full of people who were only too glad to turn them over to the authorities. The classic image was of a German pilot baling out and landing in a field, to be confronted by a farmworker with a pitchfork. It was not entirely fiction. It happened more than once.

On 8th July 1940, for example, Mrs. Nora Cardwell disarmed and captured a Luftwaffe pilot whose plane had been shot down over the northeast coast of England. She described the incident.

'One of my farm men came to the door and said some German parachutists were coming down. I went to the telephone, but found it was out of order. I told a boy to go on his bicycle for the police. But in the meantime, I had to do something myself. We had been told that we had to deal with these parachutists very quickly before they had a chance to do any damage.

'I went out into the garden and saw an airman limping hanging across the paddock near the house. There were two or three people about, but they didn't do anything, so I walked up to this young man and told him to put his hands up. He didn't understand until I made signs and then, he raised his hands in the air. I pointed to the automatic pistol he had in his belt and he gave it to me.

'He was about 6ft.3ins. tall and about twenty five years of age. I walked with him in front of me to the road. We waited for about half an hour before the police and soldiers arrived and took him away.'

One of the most unfortunate of the Luftwaffe pilots was Gefreiter Niessel who was Flight Engineer on a Junkers-88 bomber when the engines began to fail. The pilot ordered the crew to jump out, but only Niessel did so. He landed safely, but the pilot changed his mind. Realising that despite the failing engines, he had a chance to get back to Germany, he flew on and managed to reach base. The stranded Niessel was later captured near Tangmere. It had been

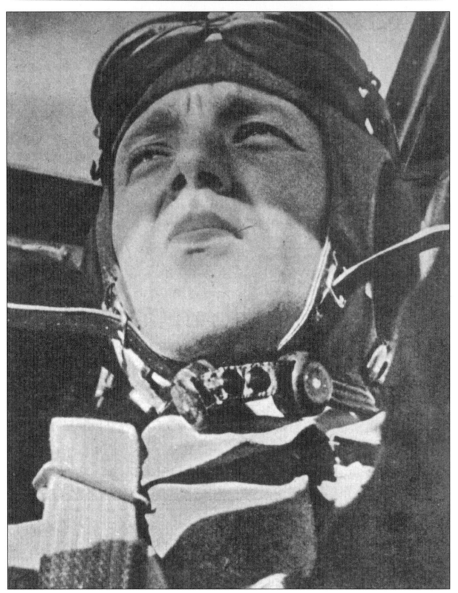

The airman has a pilot's helmet, goggles and a laryngaphone, which transmits his words directly from his larynx and permits of intercommunication between the members of the crew, in spite of the noise of the engines. That is of the utmost importance for concentration of fighting force.

his first and last flight.

The Luftwaffe's opponents, by contrast, had the luxury of operating over home territory, with a much shorter run home to their airfields and friendly faces all round if they were forced to bale out. Many of them returned immediately to base and were flying again the same day, or the next.

Despite the ferocity of combat in the Battle of Britain, it did not always occur to pilots on either side that they, not the other fellow, might be shot down and killed. The first time he went into battle, the famous pilot Richard Hillary 'felt an empty sensation of suspense in the pit of my stomach.' It was not fear for himself, but fear at the thought that he was about to kill.

Hillary found himself tangling with a Messerschmitt.

'He came right through my sights and I saw the tracer from all eight guns thud home. For a second, he seemed to hang motionless; then a jet of red flame shot upward and he spun out of sight. For the next few minutes, I was too busy looking after myself to think of anything but the rest of the enemy aircraft turned and made off over the Channel and we were ordered to our base. My mind began working again. It had happened.'

Like Hillary, Ulrich Steinhilper, an Me-109 pilot, who took part in a raid on RAF Manston in Kent on 19th August 1940, was chilled by the thought that destroying an opponent's aircraft also meant killing him.

'We roared over the coast just east of Margate and within seconds we were approaching Manston. I spotted a tanker that was refuelling a Spitfire quite close to the airfield boundary. Dropping height to about three or four metres, I saw the tanker rapidly filling my illuminated red firing ring. Increasing the pressure on the trigger and the button, I felt all four machine guns begin to fire. I saw the strikes and flashes as the bullets began to hit home and the tanker began to burn.'

Next, Steinhilper turned his attention to two Spitfires waiting nearby to be refuelled in their turn. His machine gun fire tore up the ground and then the Spitfires were hit. The tanker blew up in a ball of fire and the Spitfires began to burn. Despite the elation of success, Steinhilper knew there were men as well as machines down there.

'I was assailed by a conflict of feelings. First, I had done what I had been trained to do and done it well. It was a victory for me, and a victory for Germany. I had set fire to thousands of litres of precious fuel and left three Spitfires in ruins. But I had also seen that my attack had cost the life of at least one man and that was, and still is, hard to take.'

Ten weeks later, Steinhilper was shot down near Canterbury in Kent. He baled out safely and was imprisoned for the rest of the War.

The difficulties the Luftwaffe was encountering in the Battle of Britain tried

Goering's patience to extremes. He had very little patience in any case, for he was easily dissatisfied with anything less than quick success. As the Battle wore on into September, and the RAF showed no signs of cracking, Goering took to criticising the Luftwaffe fighter pilots for failing him and for lacking aggression. He also drove them hard, refusing to allow rest days or to rotate the front-line units so that they could refresh themselves. The pilots became tired out and disillusioned and for the first time began to doubt their own effectiveness.

It was also a matter of shame for the Luftwaffe when the much-vaunted JU-87 Stukas had to be withdrawn from the Battle because they proved too vulnerable to RAF attack. The Stukas' undoing was the very feature that had once been considered its advantage: the moment when the JU-87 positioned itself for its eighty-degree dive-bombing run, and was about to shriek down on its target below was also the moment when it was most open to attack. The Stukas suffered very heavy losses, most of which occurred as they stooped to make their dive.

The Stukas were so vulnerable that they had to be escorted by Messerschmitt-109Es. The JU-87s were very slow-flying aircraft and the Me-109s, which were superior aircraft, had to cut down on their own speed capability because of it. The Spitfires and Hurricanes were frequently waiting for them and their losses were tremendous. One Luftwaffe squadron lost its group commander, its adjutant and all three of its commanders within two weeks. This made a young lieutenant, Gunther Rall the new squadron commander and he was only 22 years old.

The Luftwaffe pilots were frustrated, too, by the serendipity of the RAF squadrons which invariably managed to be in the right place at the right time to intercept them. The explanation was the RAF's radio detection and ranging equipment - RADAR - which had already been in operational use before 1939 and was now playing its first vital defensive role in the War. Adolf Galland, the famous German fighter ace wrote:

'We realised that the RAF fighter squadrons must be controlled from the ground by some new procedure, because we heard commands skillfully and accurately directing Spitfires and Hurricanes onto the German formations...For us, this radar and fighter control was a surprise and a very bitter one.'

The Germans had RADAR themselves, and used it very effectively during the War. Horst Ramstetter was convinced the British has stolen it from them and then prevented the Germans from using it themselves.

'They blew us out of the sky after our RADAR system had been stolen by the English. Our RADAR was able to register approaching formations, to register the numbers and say what was up there. Our control room could say there are fighters in the air, they come from such and such a place. English advance troops picked up this sophisticated technology, the whole thing, from the Channel or wherever, and took it to England. The Battle of Britain was won by the English because of that. They were able to switch off our radar system, all the frequencies, so we couldn't use it. They were very sneaky lads, those English'.

Combined with their other disadvantages, German losses in the Battle of Britain, 1,733 aircraft overall to the RAF's 915, were so high that it became impossible for the Luftwaffe to carry on. It had become evident that they were not going to seize command of the air and without command of the air, there could be no invasion. On 12th October, Operation Sealion, the invasion of Britain, was postponed 'indefinitely' by Adolf Hitler. This postponement was meant to last until the following year, but the campaign was never resumed. Britain, which had not been successfully invaded for almost nine centuries, remained the only opponent still able to confront the Nazis for a year to the day, until Russia was forced into the War by the German invasion of 22nd June 1941.

Adolf Hitler never forgave Goering for the failure of Luftwaffe in the Battle of Britain. The shine had gone from its dazzling, invincible image and its reputation was never quite the same again. After the cancellation of Operation Sealion, Hitler and Goering met only when it was unavoidable and Goering contrived to keep out of the Führer's way at every possible opportunity. Some Luftwaffe pilots, just as disillusioned as their Führer, came to realise what lay behind Goering's outward bluster. One of them was Anton Heinemann.

'Yes, Goering was a great bragger. He boasted he could be called Meyer - a Jewish name - if any enemy plane flew over German territory. What nonsense! How could he have forgotten that the RAF raided the Kiel Canal and the German naval bases at Wilhelmshaven and Brunsbuttel on the second day of the War, in 1939? Besides, against the British, we never had command of the air, certainly not during the day, though the night fighters managed to function until the end of the War.'

On 10th June 1940, a few weeks before the Battle of Britain began, Il Duce Mussolini, fascist dictator of Italy, had entered the war on the German side. Italian operations were at first concentrated in Africa, where Mussolini was intent on building an empire which, he boasted, would one day rival that of the Romans. The Mediterranean, he bragged, was 'Mare Nostrum', Our Sea.

The Italians were not entirely willing combatants. When Il Duce announced his declaration of war to a large crowd in Rome, voices were heard telling him, among other epithets, to 'Drop dead!' Mussolini's ambitions in Africa prevailed, just the same, and on 4th July, the Italian forces invaded the British protectorate of Somaliland. By 13th September, the Italians were moving

An airman's equipment would be incomplete without a parachute, the life-belt of the air to which many an airman owes his life.

towards Egypt, where there was a large concentration of British forces and the vital Suez Canal. The British hit back, destroying the Italian fleet at Taranto in November 1940, and invading Italian Eritrea in January 1941. Before long, the Italians were in difficulties and Mussolini was appealing to Adolf Hitler for help. It was the first, though not the last time, that Italian ineptitude made them a liability to their German Allies.

Hitler's response was to send General Erwin Rommel and his crack Afrika Korps to help the Italians. At the same time, the Luftwaffe's Air Corps X, with five hundred aircraft, was sent from Norway to Sicily. Their principle task was to harass enemy shipping and maintain the supply lines to North Africa. The Luftwaffe also went into action in direct support of the German and Italian ground forces on 16th February 1941, when they raided the port of Benghazi, which had fallen into British hands a week earlier. By the time the Luftwaffe had finished, Benghazi was unusable as a base for the British forces in Libya.

Two months later, when the Germans rescued the Italians again by invading Greece, Luftwaffe power proved so strong that the small RAF fighter force on Crete was forced to withdraw from the fray. The Luftwaffe, for once, had command of the air and used it in intensive air raids designed to smash the British forces on Crete.

This was only the preliminary to the first major airbourne assault in military history, which was carried out by the XI Airbourne Corps in May 1940. Despite very heavy losses, the mass parachute drops continued. The losses so shocked Hitler that he never again attempted another large-scale airbourne assault, but within less than two weeks, by 31st May, the British had been forced to evacuate Crete and the island was in German hands.

An important target for the Germans in the Mediterranean was the island of Malta, a British possession strategically sited where RAF aircraft operating from its airfield could endanger the supply lines of the Afrika Korps. The Luftwaffe had already raided Malta 114 times by the first week of March 1941. Between September 1941 and June 1942, nearly 14,000 tons of bombs were dropped on the island, the maximum in a day being 500 tons and on one occasion, the anti-aircraft guns were manned continuously for sixty-six hours.

Sir Archibald Sinclair, Secretary of State for Air in the wartime coalition government, delivered a graphic report of one of these raids to the House of Commons.

'The first time the Luftwaffe raided, they came over in the afternoon in two waves. There was quite a good number of planes, too, and they kept diving over the Grand Harbour for half an hour. Then came an interval of about fifteen minutes, and they started all over again....Although the Germans had guts to come down that low, they were terrible shaken. Plane after plane zoomed over very low indeed with engines sparking and smoke coming out from wings and tail. Every imaginable anti-aircraft shell was used against them. The sky was ablaze and I was nearly deafened by bomb and shell explosions. During that engagement, the Germans lost eleven aircraft. When they returned a couple of days later, they lost another nine and next day another nineteen.'

For the Luftwaffe, Malta and in particular its capital and chief port, Valletta, was not an easy target. Hajo Herman was familiar with some of the difficulties.

'When we flew in to attack Valetta, where warships were moored, we had to fly very exactly, maintain height, course and speed with mathematic correctness so that the bomb aimer's measurements could be correct. For us, that was the critical and very dangerous moment. Down below, the flak could also measure exactly, and when they begin to drive up their barrages, then that is quite something, and you can hear it. You can see when a shell explodes in front of you, it seems quite close which it is, close to the side. You can tell from the fact that if a plane is hit, then it explodes beside you in the air. Those are very, very tricky situations - the clean, correct approach to definite targets where the ground fire is aimed exactly.'

The battle over Malta was to continue in the same punishing vein into 1942 and 1943 and the Luftwaffe also acted to bomb and strafe in best blitzkrieg style during advances by the Afrika Korps, for instance, during the battle of Kasserine Pass in February 1943. Hitler had been unenthusiastic about diverting German troops to Africa. To him, it was a sideshow that absorbed men and matériel better used elsewhere. His hand was forced, however, by the dashing, charismatic Rommel. Under Rommel's leadership, the daring exploits of the Afrika Korps made them popular heroes in Germany and the publicity and morale value of their successes were too great for even the Führer to ignore. Hitler's real interest, a very longstanding one, was the invasion and conquest of Russia.

Russia posed significant geographical problems for an invader. It was the first really extensive area the Germans had attempted to bring under their control and its vast size made it a completely different battlefield from Poland or France. Their much smaller land areas and the good 'tank country' provided by their terrain had been well suited to the swift blitzkrieg advance, while allowing the defenders little room for safe strategical withdrawal and no time for regrouping.

The Luftwaffe's style of warfare was an integral part of blitzkrieg, but Russia offered no opportunities for winning quickly by lightning war.

Not only was there too much territory to cover, but the Russians were able

The destroyer Me-110 zooms up with incredible manoeuvrability and irresistible fighting power.

THE PROPAGANDA WAR
FROM THE ENGLISH LANGUAGE VERSION OF DER ADLER

An angry armoured insect dives from the clouds - a Henschel Hs-123 during a nose dive.

Dornier Do-215 bombers thunder against the foe, like medieval heroes in armour with their visors down.

to hide away their reserves in places beyond reach. They were able, too, to disperse their weapons manufacturing facilities over a very wide area. In November 1941, for example, as the Germans neared Moscow, the city's important SKF ball-bearing factory was evacuated and set up on a new site hundreds of miles to the east.

The Germans lacked the long-range bombers needed to deal with these widely dispersed industrial centres. They were still relying on the twin-engined Heinkel 111 medium bomber which had first been used by the Condor Legion in Spain in 1938. During the Second World War, the 111 comprised the major part of the Luftwaffe's bomber arm. It could fly 1,212 miles at 205 miles per hour with a full bomb load of some 5,500 pounds, but this was a very modest range and capacity for the task of destroying the Russian arms industry.

Although the Luftwaffe never managed that, its presence in Russia was considerable. The first, second and fourth Luftflotten were deployed, comprising a total of 2,770 aircraft, more than half Germany's total front line strength. This included 775 bombers, 310 Ju-87 Stukas and 920 single- and twin-engined fighters.

Within a week of the invasion, on 29th June 1941, Adolf Hitler was already issuing so-called 'victory communiqués' detailing, inter alia, a dazzling series of Luftwaffe successes.

'The German air force delivered a crushing blow at the Russian air force. In air battles and by anti-aircraft fire on land, 4,107 Russian planes have been destroyed. In contrast to these losses are the comparatively moderate German losses of 150 planes.'

The Russian High Command countered these claims with a communiqué of their own on 30th June, putting Luftwaffe losses at 1,500 aircraft to the Russian Air Force's 850. The real figures, by the end of September, were nearer 4,500 Russian aircraft destroyed, to Luftwaffe's losses of around 2,000.

Despite the propaganda put out by both sides, the Luftwaffe certainly dealt the Russian air force some very heavy punishment. Early on in the campaign, they seized command of the air and by the end of September 1941, they had destroyed around 4,500 Russian aircraft for the loss of around 2,000 planes of their own. The Polikarpov 1-16 Rata, which gave Hajo Hermann such problems in Spain, was still the best and most numerous Russian fighter in 1941 and hundreds were destroyed on the ground when the Luftwaffe raided their airfields. In the air, the Ratas were outclassed by the Me-109s and FW-190s and many were shot down.

Karl Born had a very poor opinion of the Russian air force.

'It was very bad. The Russian pilots were cowards. They used to turn away when we came on the scene. They never attacked us, except once when we were in a Fieseler Storch. But we were able to run out the landing flaps and reduce speed, so the Russian shot past us before he could pull the trigger. The closer we were to the ground, the worse it was for him, because he had a large turning circle and couldn't follow us any more.

'There was one Russian aircraft we came to know very well. We called it the 'sewing machine'. It was an ancient double-decker which always arrived at night and hurled all sorts of stuff down, stones, bits of iron. It was all very primitive.'

Command of the air enabled the Ju-87 Stukas to fulfil their traditional role as tactical support for the German ground forces. Horst Ramstetter spent three years in Russia piloting dive-bombers.

'At the beginning of the Russian campaign, I was immediately sent into action in the last open-cockpit biplane, the Henschel-123, the forerunner of the Ju 87 Stuka. The HS 123 had an engine power of about 900 hp and it was so manoeuvrable that in the pilot's jargon 'you could turn it around a lamp post'. It was a robust plane . They shot at me from below through the lower wing into the upper wing, there was a hole that I could almost crawl through and the thing still kept flying. I think you'd have to take the wings off then it would stop flying, and not before. It was that robust.'

Ramstetter flew missions that seemed to take him back to a form of warfare from the past.

'We flew missions against mounted units at the beginning of the war in Russia. Just imagine that, the Cossacks. Horse drawn. I was up in the HS-123 when I saw some galloping horses and riders. One of them looked around and I saw his eyes, full of fear. I couldn't fire. I couldn't fire. I couldn't fire at the enemy. He suddenly became a human being for me. Why? In war, it's either you or me, that's the rule for every soldier the world over, either you or me and whoever is faster, he survives longer. But I couldn't fire, not that time.'

'I flew 300 missions in the HS 123, in the southern sector in Russia. Early on, I never got further north than Kiev in the Ukraine, but later, I flew over Stalingrad, supporting the ground troops. Afterwards, I was sent on missions all over Russia as a fighter bomber. But the HS-123 was very ancient. so I was retrained on the FW-190'

Alfred Wagner was very enthusiastic about the FW-190, which was introduced into the Luftwaffe after 1941 as a replacement for the Me-109s.

'The FW-190 was much more manoeuvrable in the air than many other aircraft. It had good loading capacity and weaponry and the technical standard was very high. It was also faster and had the advantage of being able to evade other planes quite easily. It swerved away beautifully, and was marvellously manoeuvrable - not as much as the Spitfire, of course, but a great improvement

A Heinkel fighter shows its manoeuvrability in a steep turn.

Work now begins in earnest. The formalities of acceptance have been completed, the Do-215 is ready to take off, and the first flight to the front airdrome will soon begin.

on what we'd had before.'

In 1942, an FW-190 on patrol along the Norwegian coast sited a large convoy heading through the arctic seas towards Murmansk. The convoy was carrying vital supplies for the Russians: armour plate, steel, nickel, oil, aluminium, cordite, TNT, aircraft parts, guns, planes and food cargoes. For six days, the Luftwaffe strove to prevent the ships reaching port and the battle was of mammoth proportions.

One Heinkel bomber flew through a hail of fire from one of the corvette escorts and dropped a torpedo that blasted a huge hole in the engine room of one ship, which had to be abandoned. Soon afterwards, twenty-four twin-engined Luftwaffe bombers came in at no more than 30 feet above sea level. Nineteen failed to get through the defensive fire, but the other five torpedoed three vessels.

Hajo Hermann describes the so-called 'Turnip' technique, the Schtekrübe, which the Luftwaffe used to sink ships.

'If you attack a steamer in order to sink it, then mostly you drop the bomb down either horizontally or so that it descends almost vertically and strikes amidships, or in the funnel if possible, or by diving or gliding towards the ship and then releasing it. But there was another technique contrived by people who believed it was not possible to sink a ship by striking it from above because there is so much junk lying around on deck. Sometimes there are armoured tanks and the bomb explodes in the tank, but the ship doesn't sink. 'With the 'Turnip' technique, you flew in very low , diagonally towards the ship's side, and released the bomb when you're very close. The bomb goes tearing into the side of the ship and rips open a huge hole. The water floods in and the ship sinks. Of course the 'turnip' technique involved enormous risk because the men on deck could see an attacker coming slowly in straight at the target, so they fire at him with precision and can hit him very easily.'

An eyewitness on board one of the ships in the convoy later described the experience of being attacked from the air by the Luftwaffe.

'We had six days of almost constant bombing raids. Our escort ships put up a magnificent barrage, but the German pilots came right through it and gave us all they had. A catapult plane on our ship was shot off to meet the attackers. The pilot, a young South African, took off to break up the Luftwaffe formation. We saw him bring down a large bomber and then go off to chase another. But a signal reached our ship that the pilot was wounded and had been forced to bale out. He jumped clear of the machine and made a perfect parachute drop into the sea. A destroyer went to his rescue and got him safely on board.

On the following day, a direct hit was made on our vessel. She immediately began to sink. Two boats were launched. One was only an oar's length from the

A large "Condor" airplane of the type Fw-200 is given start permission.

ship when a bomb blew it to pieces, killing five men. In the other boat, we had to lie down on our faces during a machine-gun attack by a German plane. Luckily, none of us was injured, but our boat was shattered. We found ourselves in the freezing water, clinging to driftwood. We were not left long in the water. The rescue ship did magnificent work, ignoring risks to save our lives.

'There was never any darkness to give protection from attacks. We were too far north for that and it was summer, when daylight was perpetual. Every man in the convoy had to be on duty throughout the six days and so-called nights without thought of rest or sleep.'

Attacking the convoys was not as easy as it might have appeared, as Hajo Hermann realised when he targeted an aircraft carrier in the arctic waters.

'It was up in the Polar sea, and the prevailing weather was heavy snow showers with very clear intervals. The British had an aircraft carrier cruising around, covering a convoy that was sailing there. I flew beneath the clouds towards the aircraft carrier -you could see for a great distance from beneath the clouds if there wasn't a snow shower. I pulled up high, staying very close to the clouds because I always had to reckon with the fighters from the aircraft carrier climbing up and shooting me down.

'I thought, if the carrier sails into an area of blue, completely clear weather and sunshine, then you are in a dreadful situation. For this reason I thought, when this aircraft carrier comes out from beneath the next shower, that will be the right moment for me to dive down the cloud wall, when the carrier's snout is just emerging, and then I'll drop the bombs in the middle. That, at least, was my plan.

'At the moment I began to dive there was clear visibility and I was fired at heavily from the bow of the carrier. As I dived, it came further and further out and then the English let loose such a violent barrage in front of us, that they hit my right hand engine. It wasn't disabled but they'd shot through the rods. I had both engines idling during the dive so that I wouldn't be too fast, and this engine with the damaged rods was now running at full speed.

'The plane spun away and I couldn't stop it, couldn't keep on target and my bomb, an armour-piercing bomb weighing 1,400 Kg fell about 5 metres from the ship. It was so terribly difficult to get close to those aircraft carriers.'

In Russia, the conditions under which the Luftwaffe had to operate were appalling. When the fearsome Russian winter closed in, pilots found their radios refused to work. The weather hampered accurate intelligence gathering. Aircraft coming in to land skidded off the runways, with the result that the Luftwaffe was able to operate at only one quarter of its strength. There were just as many planes lost through accidents as were lost in combat. The antiquated Russian air force which had been so easily destroyed at the start of the campaign had been replaced by modern aircraft which,even before the start of winter, made the Russians twice as strong in the air as the Luftwaffe.

At the beginning of 1942 an extra strain was put on the Luftwaffe after the first major Russian offensive of the War attempted to push the Germans back along the entire 2,000-mile front. Despite the seas of mud of the notorious Rasputitza, caused by the autumn rains of 1941 followed by one of the worst winters even Russia had seen, the Germans had managed to advance into the suburbs of Moscow by the end of the year. The Russian winter offensive of 1942 ensured that they got no further. The pressure was taken off Moscow as the north-south battle line in the vicinity of the capital was forced back and the German salients came under threat. For the Luftwaffe, Moscow was a dangerous area. The capital was ringed with mighty - and accurate - anti-aircraft batteries and the toll of German planes was such that their last raid, on the night of 24th October1941, was carried out by only eight aircraft.

The Luftwaffe was called in to airlift supplies to the beleaguered German units on the ground, but there were too few available personnel. To fill the gaps, flying instructors and students from the air training schools were drafted in as pilots for the Junkers-52s, the capacious tri-motor freighter aircraft. The Russians did not achieve all their objectives. Besieged Sevastopol and Kharkov remained in German hands, but the invaders were thrown out of Rostov, near the Sea of Azov, and thrust back a distance of 120 miles.

Long before this, according to Adolf Hitler, the forces of the Third Reich should have home, dry and victorious. Instead, they found themselves still battling the mammoth of Russian resistance, which as yet, showed no signs of weakening let alone collapsing. German prospects brightened, however, after June 1942 when the Caucasus proved to be a weak link in the Russian defences. The Germans managed to relieve their forces inside besieged Sevastopol and organised Russian resistance in the Crimea came to an end.

Horst Ramstetter had flown in support of the German ground forces and personally experienced the ferocity of the Russian resistance.

'The fighter bombers had to fly low, we had to support the attacking troops, our troops, destroy supply positions, destroy tanks, bomb troop positions, those were our tasks. We flew down at house height immediately in the range of the Russian guns, which of course then raked us with fire. I was shot down, as I pulled up the plane it began to burn, I couldn't bail out with the parachute, so I set my HS-123 down on the ground at an angle.

'The undercarriage sheered off, so I couldn't land properly. But I managed to get down and leapt out of the plane before it burst into flames. I was wearing the flying overalls, so the heat only burned me a little. I leapt into a shell hole.

Everything boomed and whistled, I felt so miserable, completely alone. Then, a tank rolled up, a German tank. 'Hey pilot,' I heard someone say. 'Come here' I said 'I can't, they're shooting.' The tank drove up, I jumped up onto it and went through the whole tank attack. I was never so afraid as I was in that tank.'

Ramstetter went on other dangerous missions and once came down to land in 'no man's land' between the Russian and German lines. A fierce battle was taking place at the time.

'There were certain mission targets that were, shall I say, dangerous, heavy concentration of flak, of troops, there were flak tanks sent against us, and I fell between Russian and German troops in the front line and sat in a shell hole. I put my head up and thought 'They were all firing at me! They couldn't be firing at anyone else.' 'Hallo, hallo' I heard; 'Come here, come here.' It was an infantryman, a sniper from the German lines, who came leaping over to me because I was stuck there and must have made an impression of helplessness. We called these men the 'Frozen Meat Award Warriors', the corporals, they were the hard-bitten men, nothing touched them, they were unshakeable. 'He said 'come here'. I said, 'I can't they're shooting.' He said 'I'll come to you. Look, we'll jump from here to there to there.' I said: 'Where?' 'Over to our lines.' I said, 'through that firing?' 'Look' he said 'I'll go first and you follow.' Then he called 'Where are you?' and I said 'The firing is so heavy, I can't just run through it.' I finally got over with the corporal and was glad that I was in the German position and had some cover.'

The prime purpose of the Germans' 1942 campaign in the Caucasus was the capture of Stalingrad which was strategically sited on the River Volga. In German hands, Stalingrad, one of the foremost Russian industrial centres, would open the way into Astrakhan, an important terminus of rail and river communication for the south. The Russians' supply of petroleum would be drastically reduced and they would be unable to use Stalingrad as a jumping off point for a new offensive in the winter of 1942-1943. The Germans now expected to consolidate their conquest of the Caucasus as a prelude to winning the war in Russia.

The Russians were well aware of what the fall of Stalingrad would mean to them, and in late August 1942, when the German Sixth Army attacked from the northwest and the Fourth Panzer Army from the southwest, the Russian 62nd Army under General Vasili Chuikov was ordered to stop them, no matter what the cost. He had every intention of doing so. 'Every German soldier,' Chuikov remarked 'must be made to feel that he is living under the muzzle of a Russian gun.' In the event, the cost to the Russians was enormous, but to the Germans, it was infinitely greater.

THE PROPAGANDA WAR
FROM THE ENGLISH LANGUAGE VERSION OF DER ADLER

The World War airman, the young officer of the new German Air Force, and two young lads of the Flieger-Hitler-Jugend (Aviation Section of the Hitler Youth).

THE DEFEAT OF THE LUFTWAFFE
1943-1944

The battle for Stalingrad is frequently cited as the bloodiest, most hard-fought and most destructive struggle of the Second World War and for the Luftwaffe's part in this monumental contest was always gruelling. They played many roles, not only attacking targets, but carrying out reconnaissance and patrols, gathering information and airlifting supplies. Hermann Goering's boastful opinion of his Luftwaffe had remained unchanged and when the Sixth Army was encircled and trapped inside Stalingrad in late November 1942, he assured Hitler that the air force was able to provide the supplies needed to sustain the Germans and enable them to keep on fighting. The amount required was about 550 tons a day. It proved to be an impossible target, given the ferocity of Russian anti-aircraft activity. The end result was the near-destruction of the Luftwaffe's transport arm.

In these circumstances, any role the Luftwaffe might play on any particular day was dangerous and nerve-wracking. Horst Ramstetter considers his missions at Stalingrad were the hardest he ever flew in his entire career as and airman.

'Undoubtedly, the most difficult mission was Stalingrad, because the concentration of defences was so enormous, more than at any time from beginning to the end of the Russian campaign. For me at any rate, it was an enormous effort to reach the various points that had been chosen as targets there, fly there and do the job.'

The job entailed pounding Stalingrad with such damaging raids that the water mains were destroyed and large areas of the city were left burning. Many of the buildings had to be pulled down to stop the blaze spreading. Dar Gova, in the south of Stalingrad near the River Volga, was obliterated, leaving its rows of neat bungalows a mess of smoking wood and ash. At the nearby sugar plant, now in ruins, only the grain elevator remained standing.

Before the battle began, the younger German airmen had not realised what they were in for. Horst Ramstetter remembers the excitement and anticipation of 18-year olds facing their first battle, and how quickly these feelings changed.

'When our advance on Stalingrad began, everyone said, great, we're moving, marching, everything's fine. Then they realised too late that the Russians had no intention of losing. To them, Stalingrad was a sort of 'show town', an object of prestige. Some of the pilots were only eighteen and had never flown a mission. They'd had their heads filled with 'Führer, Volk and Vaterland - we'll storm onwards, we heroes will win the war!'. But the real thing was very different. They came back crying their eyes out. They were ready to drop, they hadn't been prepared for such an operation, or for an enemy as ferocious as the Russians. The raw reality pulled them back down to the earth.'

Ramstetter remembers how he discovered that the Russians had broken through the German defences.

'Romanian troops, our Allies, were fighting with our forces. They were positioned to the north of Stalingrad. Two of us flew a mission over the area. We were supposed to find out what was going on because the front line was a bit confused. I looked down and saw these greyish-brown uniforms. The Romanians! I thought, and decided to check it out.

'I dived down, but I was fired at. I said, 'Those crazy Rumanians, why are they firing at us, we're -.' It wasn't the Romanians, it was the Russians but what were they doing there? I immediately flew back to base at Pitomnik and reported: the Russians have broken through. Where? I showed them where on the map. 'That's impossible,' they said 'That's where the Rumanians are. Yes, exactly there, I said. And once the reconnaissance had flown over and confirmed my report, we prepared the airstrip ready for defence.

'We knew if the Russians kept advancing like that, that they'd be on top of us in a day. We had nothing, no infantry, nothing. We had already been forced to evacuate our airfield, because the Russians were too near. Now, they were coming close again and all we could do was sit in the trenches and wait until they arrived. We lay there all night and at first light, at dawn, we climbed into the planes and flew up over the airstrip. The Russians were already there, and they fired on us.

'We flew fifteen or sixteen missions. We were reloaded with ammunition and bombs whilst the engines were still running and then we had to take off again.'

By October 1942, the battle for Stalingrad had already become a battle of attrition. Russian resistance was so fanatical that General Paulus, in command of the German Sixth Army, lost four battalions in exchange for capturing a block of flats. On 14th October, five German divisions were sent to overrun two factories, supported by three thousand sorties from the Luftwaffe.

In December 1942, Horst Ramstetter's squadron was transferred to Nichechieskaya, south of Stalingrad. They wanted to celebrate Christmas with a sing-song but instead found themselves in the thick of battle.

'We heard: 'Alarm! Alarm! The Russians have broken through'. Thank God

The Fw-87 Flying upside-down. The clean-cut lines of this modern destroyer plane show that it can complete with any antagonist in speed and manoeuvrability.

Destroyer formation on the wing. The powerful engines and a copious supply of fuel give this type of airplane a wide radius of action.

we had an 88 flak unit with us, one that had been pulled back from the front. The 88 was the best anti-tank gun of all, although it had been intended as an anti aircraft gun. But it kept the Russians off our necks and we were able to take off and fly over Stalingrad which was already under siege. Army Group South were supposed to relieve the Sixth Army with their advance tanks. We thought, great, thank God! But it didn't work out that way.

'General Paulus, with his 150,000 soldiers, sat there in Stalingrad. The supply lines weren't working. They'd been told 'The Luftwaffe can supply you, you can hold out. But that didn't work. They went hungry, they had no ammunition no fuel, and they ate the horses that were lying around dead. We saw the front line of the relieving army and saw the signals from the besieged pocket. The distance between them was 40 kilometres.

'The men on the ground had been told: 'When a German soldier stands there, he does not yield one centimetre of ground'. These stupid orders, the glorification of heroism. Madness! Suddenly the relieving army halted. What's wrong now, we wondered? I'll tell you: the Russians broke through the southern wing and soon Russians and Germans were fighting house to house. Sometimes they were on different floors. When we flew attacks on Stalingrad, we couldn't tell our troops from the Russians.'

For Ramstetter, total war on the ground at Stalingrad was translated to total war in the air.

'We carried many injured men, picked them up directly from the from the medical stations near the front lines, we flew very close to the front, but at low level. We were often able to avoid the flak because we knew roughly where the flak batteries were. But over Stalingrad we used to fly very low because the light flak, which was operated by women, was very accurate and low flying meant they couldn't track us so easily.

'The heavy flak was quite a different matter. The Russians had set up their flak, and before you got to the Stalingrad, you saw what looked like a wall of fire. Shells detonated, it looked like darker and lighter balls of cotton wool. And we had to fly into them! There wasn't time to be afraid because we were so preoccupied with keeping our planes in the air, but when I returned to base, I felt I had just been dragged across an obstacle course. We didn't have much respite, though. We were soon in the air again, to reconnoitre the Russian troops' supplies.

On one such mission, disaster nearly overtook Ramstetter after his aircraft was shot down. He narrowly escaped the Germans' worse fear in Russia, being captured by the communists.

'I was flying an FW-190, and discovered a Russian train loaded with war material. We attacked and destroyed the engine, but my aircraft received a massive hit and I had to make an emergency landing. I came down behind the Russian lines.

'We carried emergency rations of a bar of choco-cola and weather proof matches and Dextrose. We had the machine gun on board the plane and were carrying our own hand guns. I got out of the plane, saw a corn field and ran into it. I heard the troops rolling past somewhere in the distance and I said to myself: 'If the Russians should come now, you've got seven or eight rounds in your gun. You can try to get the Ivans with seven of them and the last one you've got left will be for yourself.' But I thought again and said: 'Nothing doing! I'm not going to kill myself.'

'I had my compass with me and knew in which direction I had to go. I set off, always keeping myself hidden. On the second night, I arrived at a German border position on the front line. I swam across a river and ran across a field and shouted, 'Don't shoot! I'm a German pilot!' But just as I reached the position safely, a Russian fighter-bomber appeared and dived down on us. Everyone threw themselves to the ground and some men jumped on top of me. They saved my life. They were hit by shrapnel, but I survived, but I thought, I'd rather volunteer for 100 combat missions than go through another day like this.'

Aerial combat with the Russian fighters was a traumatic experience for Detlef Radbruch.

'It's an awful moment to see six planes fly towards you all at once. It was frightening. We didn't know what was going to happen. But when you were fighting, operating the gun and firing it and hitting your opponent were the only things that mattered. When we had flown difficult missions, we called it birthday celebrations, we celebrated our birthday, for having got through it.

'We flew in formations of up to five planes and each had three machine guns. We had agreed on the tactic of firing at the first Russian plane that approached us and mostly we managed to shoot it down or damage it badly so that it turned away. When that happened, the other five Russians turned away as well. Except, that is for the pilot we called 'the Commissar'. You always knew there was a fanatical communist piloting that plane, because he'd attack us even though we outnumbered him. We were hit many times. Once, our undercarriage was hit so that we had to land on one wheel and make a crash landing. Fortunately, all of us got out in one piece.

'We were very lucky, but many others weren't. It's a terrible thing to see a comrade shot down. During transport flights over the Kuban bridgehead in the Caucasus, we had escort planes. They kept the Russian fighter planes at a distance but several of them were shot down. When we saw that, it was a great shock every time. At Stalingrad, some 488 planes were shot down and more than one thousand airmen were lost. It had taken a long time to train them - a year for radio operators and about as long for pilots, but all that could be lost within a few minutes.'

Despite all the efforts of Detlef Radbruch and other German pilots, the 550 tons a day the encircled Sixth Army had been promised by Goering never materialised. It was difficult enough for the Luftwaffe to deliver 100 tons a day, and even that was rarely achieved. The transports were frequently ambushed by Russian fighters, which had special orders to destroy German supply aircraft flying to Stalingrad. On 24th November, four days before the Russians completed their encirclement of the Sixth Army, Luftflotten 4 lost twenty two out of forty-seven of their Ju-52s. Another nine were destroyed the following day. General Baron Wolfram von Richthofen, a cousin of the famous 'Red Baron', realised the how crucial this rate of loss was: 'We simply have not got the transport aircraft to do it,' he said. By December, losses among the Luftwaffe transports had risen to thirty percent of all flights attempted.

The Luftwaffe fighters, too, came under threat and Richthofen was forced to move some of his fighters into Stalingrad in order to protect them. He admitted: 'We have not been able to master the Russian fighters absolutely and, of course, the Russians can attack our forward airfields any time they like. We have been able to fly in only 75 tons instead of the 300 tons we were ordered to deliver.'

Richthofen had only 550 bombers, 350 fighters, 100 reconnaissance planes and his few transports against the Russians' 1,250 planes. The standard of servicing was low and the intense cold damaged the fabric of the aircraft, causing many of them to crash. Supply lanes that managed to land safely were plastered on the ground by Russian artillery and roving T-34 tanks and bombed and strafed by Russian fighters. Unloading them had to be done at speed, the wounded were embarked and the aircraft would have to run the gauntlet again to take off safely. The casualties in men and aircraft were massive and Pitomnik, the principle supply field for Stalingrad, was full of bomb craters, snow and wrecked planes.

Despite all this, Goering's orders to supply the troops inside Stalingrad with 500 tons a day or more still stood. Richthofen realised the part played by ego and politics in Goering's refusal to see sense.

'Orders are orders and we'll do our best to carry them out,' he commented. 'But the tragedy is that no local commander on the spot, even those who enjoy the Führer's confidence, can any longer exercise influence. As things are, we commanders, from the operations point of view, are now nothing more than highly paid NCO'S.'

When he first arrived in Russia, Detlef Radbruch worked at the direction

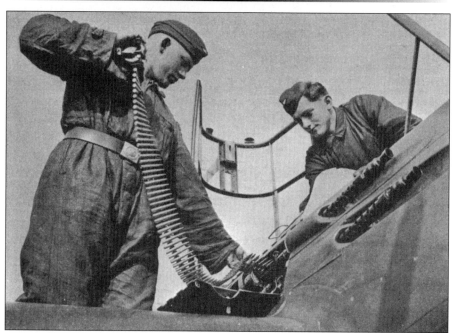

Preparations for the next take-off; the armourer is fitting ammunition belts into the machine-gun drums

Front view of the Fw-187 destroyer, showing the arrangement of the machine-guns at each side of the pilot's seat.

finding station that regulated the air traffic supplying the German pocket at Stalingrad, but he had been told he should get some flying experience, and at the end of January 1943, he flew with a night mission over the city.

'The pilot of our aircraft had already flown eleven missions to Stalingrad, so that was a lot of practice and we were going to be very grateful for it. But it was extremely dangerous, the temperatures were below minus 30, and the distance to the airfield at Stalingrad was over 300 kilometres, so it was going to be a big effort to return to base.

'The Russians had set up very powerful flak around the Sixth Army in the pocket at Stalingrad. General Paulus had already surrendered, but there was a detachment to the north of Stalingrad still holding out. We reached it and dropped our cargo - bread in sacks, sausage and ammunition. One crate, containing special ammunition got jammed in the door and the parachute dropped out and opened. Two of us were able to cut the parachute free but it became entangled in the tail fin aileron and the pilot had to struggle to keep the plane flying. Because he was an excellent and experienced pilot, he was able to get us back to the airstrip. This was the last aircraft supplying the Sixth Army at Stalingrad.

'Many of us thought the disaster at Stalingrad was Goering's fault.

'We didn't think a great deal of him. At Stalingrad there were between 260 and over 300,000 German soldiers Our planes brought out 40,000 wounded but at least 160,000 fell during the battle, and about 100,000 were taken prisoner. Only about 6,000 came home after the War. The Russian losses at Stalingrad were double or three times ours. They lost over half a million soldiers. In that dreadful battle, over half a million young people or more died because of the madness of two dictators - Hitler and Stalin.'

General Paulus surrendered in Stalingrad on 31st January 1943, and the following July, the Germans attempted to recompense themselves with the massive tank assault on the Russians at Kursk. They were beaten again and weakened their already fragile position on the eastern front. The Luftwaffe, flying in support, was hammered by the Russians and lost 1,400 aircraft. After that, Horst Ramstetter recalls, many planes were grounded due to lack of supplies.

'We'd been given all sorts of promises, about wonder weapons and miracle armaments, but it was all nonsense. What actually happened was that our supply line broke down and we couldn't get off the ground. We had to leave the planes standing, or blow them up because we didn't have any fuel.'

A scarcely less violent struggle was continuing in the Mediterranean, where the Luftwaffe were striving to keep the supplies lines open to the Afrika Korps. This imposed so much strain on the Luftwaffe pilots that one of them, a sergeant by the name of Mosbach, lost his nerve. He told his commander, Hajo Hermann, that he had decided not to fly.

'We'd been fighting against the Royal Navy and the battles were very hard. RAF fighter planes were there as well, and everyone was under terrible pressure. This Mosbach was a very capable, skilful pilot but one day he came up to me and said. "Sir, I have to report that I don't feel well, I think I'm going to be shot down on this mission." I replied, "Have you gone off your head? What's the matter with you? You're not an old woman." "No," he said, "I know that I'm making myself a laughing stock, but I have such a strong feeling, that I just can't do it today."

'I just stared at him for a bit and said, "Well, Mosbach, I've known you for a long time and I've never experienced anyone like you come up to me in this way." I was a bit angry, but I told him: "Stay at home then!" So he stayed at home. But he was shot down during another mission and floated around in a rubber dinghy until the British came and picked him up. But the terrible thing was, he was badly burned and lost his sight.'

On 9th May 1943, the German and Italian troops in Tunisia surrendered unconditionally and Erwin Rommel, the original commander of the Afrika Korps, was said to be relieved that his men were now Allied prisoners and far beyond the reach of Adolf Hitler, who would have sacrificed them rather than capitulate. The last German resistance in North Africa, at Cape Bon, was extinguished on 12th May, when, together with his entire staff, Colonel-General Jürgen von Arnim, commander of Army Group Africa was captured at an inland camp on the peninsula.

The invasion of Sicily took place on 10th July, preceded by one hundred sorties by American Mustang fighter-bombers. They bombed and strafed behind the German defence lines, plastered troop concentrations with cannon-fire and left transport, bridges, locomotives, railway yards and barracks burning and in ruins.

The Luftwaffe was now subjected to the same treatment they had meted out in Poland or Russia. The Allied air presence, which included attacks by Liberator bombers, was so overwhelming that German pilots were unable to get their planes off the ground and within only a few hours, the Allies had command of the air. The Sicilian campaign ended with the Axis surrender on 17th August 1943 and less than two weeks later, Allied forces invaded Italy.

After his service in Russia, Detlef Radbruch flew missions in Italy in support of the German troops on Sicily and as preparation for the invasion of the mainland.

'We were withdrawn from Russia and flew on special orders to southern Italy, where we were to bring the Division Hermann Goering, an infantry

THE AIRCRAFT IN RETROSPECT: DO-17

Often referred to as the Fliegender Bleistift ("flying pencil"), this was a very common light bomber or Schnellbomber, which was designed to be so fast that it could outrun opposing fighter aircraft. Equipped with two radial engines, mounted on a "shoulder wing" structure this ungainly aircraft featured a Twin tail vertical stabilizer configuration. Designed in the early 1930s, it was one of the three main Luftwaffe bomber types used in the first three years of the war. The Do-17 made its combat debut in 1937 during the Spanish Civil War, operating in the Condor Legion. Along with the Heinkel He-111 it was the main bomber type available to the Luftwaffe in 1939-40. The Dornier was popular with its crews due to its manoeuvrability and ease of handling. Its sleek and thin airframe made it harder to hit than other German bombers, due to the fact that it presented a relatively small target.

The Do-17 was phased out from front line service from 1942 onwards, as its bomb load and range were too limited. It was discovered however that the Do-17 made a very efficient reconnaissance aircraft and performed well as a night fighter, being capable of carrying bulky radar equipment, but still left room for some very heavy offensive weaponry. Some 10,000 of all types of Do-17 saw service with the Luftwaffe.

General der Flieger (Air Vice Marshal) Friedrich Christiansen, still takes his seat at the joy-stick of his Messerschmitt "Taifun" and presents a brilliant example of German flying spirit to the youth of the country.

division that was part the Luftwaffe, to Naples. After the surrender in North Africa, we flew around Italy for three weeks, bringing troops to Sicily and Sardinia because the Allied landing on Sicily was expected.'

One day, Radbruch was on the airfield at Naples Cappodiccino when he heard and 'unbelievable' sound of engines. He looked up and saw sixteen Me-323 Gigant troop transports above him. The size and capacity of the Me-323s was reflected in their name. The Gigant, which flew on six engines, had a length of just over 92 feet, and could carry 130 troops and 21,500 lbs. of freight, three times the capacity of the Junkers-52. Despite their formidable appearance, they were far from impregnable. Gigants were slow-flying and vulnerable and in April 1943, during the last days of the war in Africa, a Polish Fighter Wing serving with the RAF had downed most of a flight of twenty Gigants and sank tons of much-needed supplies into the Mediterranean. The Gigants Radbruch saw were going to meet a similar fate.

'I saw these planes and immediately thought, 'Oh God, that's not going to work, because the Allied air superiority is too great. In the evening after an Italian flight, I returned and went into the casino, A captain sat at the bar shaking his head and getting drunk: he had seen the death of the Gigants. All of them had been shot down. Each Gigant was carrying 20 tonnes of fuel, which was to be taken to Tunis. The captain said that he saw the sea burning, he was very shocked.'

Detlef Radbruch had his own dangers to face in Italy.

'We fetched German troops from Livorno and brought them to Sicily and Sardinia. These flights were very dangerous. We had to fly very low because many of our aircraft were being shot down at that time. The twin-engined Lightnings found our Junkers all too easy to destroy. We flew very, very low, because the fighters can't operate down there, and apart from that, we hoped that if we flew over the sea and were hit we could make an emergency landing in the water and be saved.'

In Italy, the Luftwaffe scored a surprise success on the night of 2-4th December 1943, when 105 Ju-88s attacked the Adriatic port of Bari, where the First British Airborne Division was based during the transfer of Allied Forces from Sicily. The attack was entirely unsuspected. There had been no attempt to blackout the port. The docks were brilliantly lit as the Luftwaffe swooped in on the thirty ships in port, and blew up two ammunition ships which caused the loss of another seventeen vessels.

One of these, the John Harvey was carrying a secret supply of mustard gas as insurance against the chance that the Germans might resort to gas warfare. The John Harvey blew up in a massive fireball that threw debris and her deadly cargo hundreds of feet into the air. The crew died instantly, and among the rest

THE PROPAGANDA WAR
FROM THE ENGLISH LANGUAGE VERSION OF DER ADLER

Powerful formations of German bombers raided the enemy and several raids on a single day, favoured by good weather all through, were nothing uncommon.

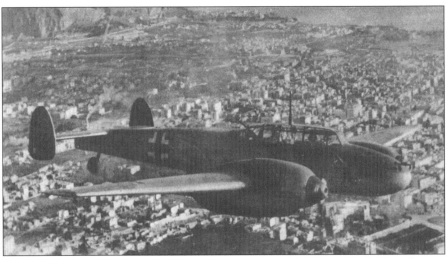

A Messerschmitt destroyer of the Me-110 type circles over Palermo, the Sicilian city.

of the estimated one thousand casualties, more than half, 628 people, died of mustard gas poisoning. Large areas of Bari were reduced to rubble, and the capacity of the port was severely curtailed for the next three weeks.

The raid on Bari resulted in supply shortages to the Allied Fifth Army in Italy and the losses sustained there prevented the US Fifteenth Air Force from participating in raids on Germany for another two months. However, the raid was not a sign of renaissance for the Luftwaffe. It was more of a final sting in the tail of a once-deadly scorpion. The Luftwaffe was, in fact, in a desperately decimated state by the time the Allies invaded Italy. There was a serious decline in number of pilots and their effectiveness naturally suffered. The Luftwaffe retained its esprit de corps and its camaraderie, but these were small advantages compared to the enormity of the task facing them after 1943. Preserving their planes and pilots became an important consideration. Horst Ramstetter was one Luftwaffe pilot who had to judge whether or not it was wise to attack.

'We had to think about whether the risk we were taking was worth it and what would happen if an attack went wrong. Sometimes we'd attack a position four times and blaze away at it with everything we had. The problem then was that the enemy fighters arrived, and our weapons went 'Click!' - there was no ammunition left.

'After that you had to start thinking about whether you'd get back to home base or not. There was, though, a trick we used to use. We called it the 'pilot's fart'. There was a stopper that you could pull out and you got extra burst of speed through an additional injection of fuel and went 40 or 50 kms. faster. The snag was that when you had pulled that thing, it virtually destroyed the engine. You could fly for perhaps five minutes and then it was over. But in an emergency, you hoped that the five minutes enabled you to escape.'

In spite of such ploys, the situation of the Luftwaffe worsened steadily.

'The pilot training periods were reduced, and because the new fighter pilots had no experience, they were the first to be shot down. As the War went on, we were no longer capable of flying missions over manufacturing plants while at the same time, Allied bombing raids on Germany were hurting us a lot.'

One important setback for the Luftwaffe was that the Allied planes had made the Me-109s obsolete. Not only was it outclassed, but the version introduced at the end of 1942, the Me-109G, carried so much firepower and extra equipment for protection against Allied attack that it was unable to operate successfully. The Luftwaffe's operational strength fell to a mere 4,000 aircraft, with no reserves. From there, the numbers fell consistently, leaving the Germans no more than 1,800 aircraft during the rest of the War. Besides this, the Allied bombing campaign on Germany reduced the Luftwaffe to a defensive role, something for which it had never been designed.

The Allied raids went on round the clock. The United States Army Air Force Flying Fortresses and Royal Air Force Lancaster bombers took turns, the first bombing Germany by day and the second, bombing by night. The cities as well as the factories of the Fatherland were targets. The Luftwaffe was short of night-bombers, and the JU-88, built as a light bomber, had to be specially adapted to cope. Heinz Philip was a gunner with one of these JU-88s.

'As the night fighting became acute, when the English started to come more and more frequently at night - we didn't have any planes specifically for the night. At first the ME 110 was equipped and put into operation as a night fighter but it couldn't fly for long enough and didn't carry enough guns, so in order to be able to use more weapons the JU 88 was used. Trials with other planes were made, but they proved ineffective.

'We didn't carry bombs. When the plane was constructed there was a space intended to house bombs and this space was filled with a tank, an additional tank so that we were able to keep flying for four hours.

'I sat at the guns on the Ju-88. There were four 2cm guns at the front and the magazines were in such a position that I could remove them when they had been emptied, that was my job, and I had to fix new magazines to the back. That was something to occupy me, but I didn't do it continuously. And when the English or the Americans attacked, that was during the day, they defended themselves and I looked at them head on. To look head on at a machine gun that is firing at you, that made me very nervous, and the pilot was busy with his plane whilst I just sat beside him and didn't know what to do. That happened the first time, but the second time I took my camera with me and from then on when we flew during the day, I took photographs so that I had something to do, to distract myself.'

Hannau Rittau served on one of the Luftwaffe anti-aircraft batteries defending Berlin from the Allied raids.

'Our battery had four guns, one range finder and one radar. There were about six people operating each gun, another six to operate the range finger and five on the radar. Our job was to protect the Heinkel aircraft factory at Oranienburg, a suburb in the north of Berlin. The light-anti aircraft couldn't come into action at all because the Allied airplanes flew far too high. We couldn't reach them because we could fire no higher than 3,500 metres or thereabouts. But the planes usually came over at almost twice that height - around 6,000 metres and only the heavy anti-aircraft could deal with them.

'Berlin was bombed almost every night, well, perhaps not every night but very regularly. The worst of it came in 1944, when the Allies started their thousand-bomber raids and one thousand of them came over at one time. The

The He-111 ready for its nocturnal trip and the crew are aboard. One engine is already running, the other will start in a moment.

Hard at work in the operations room.

The finished Ju-87 hangs as lightly as a toy from the steel cables of the crane.

sky filled with planes and during these raids, I was at my range finder. I had to pick up the aeroplanes, and get all the data which was transferred to the guns so that they could fire at the aeroplanes at the right height. There was no time for training. We learned on the job.

'Our battery was on the outskirts of Berlin Most of the anti-aircraft guns were on the outskirts, except for two anti-aircraft towers which were located right in Berlin, one of them at the Zoo. Berlin looked very, very damaged, houses came down and collapsed in ruins. But you got used to that after a while, you get used to everything after while. But we didn't like getting it every night, that was horrible.'

The raids on Berlin normally started at around 2200 hours and Rittau's anti-aircraft was alerted by radio.

'We were told where the bombers were, and were in action for three or four hours as they unloaded their bombs. Unfortunately, our flak wasn't very effective. Our battery shot down in total of eight planes which wasn't much considering how many raiders there were. We used to put a ring on our guns for every aircraft we shot down.

'We thought of the pilots up above us and wondered how they felt, being fired at. I don't suppose it felt very good when you sit in an aircraft and see all this firing going on around you and know the next one shell might hit your plane. I think that we damaged some of the planes and didn't think they would get back to England. Some of them came down over the Netherlands or in France. On the other hand, we were the ones being bombed, so we were very glad when we were able to shoot down an Allied plane.'

Rittau's world during a raid was a world of noise and flames.

'You hear a humming sound all the time - that comes from the bombers flying overhead. We used to watch through binoculars to see when the bombs came down. Of course, you could figure out roughly where they were going to fall and sometimes, if it looked too close, you had to dig in, duck your head. and pray you weren't hit. It was terrible, I mean it was a terrible noise, you would see flames over the place. We were scared, no question, all of us, but fortunately our battery was never hit by a bomb.'

Hajo Hermann was flying over Berlin in his Me-109 on 24th August 1943, while one of the Allied raids was going on. The raid was not a surprise, for Air Chief Marshal Arthur 'Bomber' Harris had already announced it. The Germans were well aware that Harris' strategy was to win the War by bombing them into submission - a mistake Hermann Goering had already made about the British during the Battle of Britain. Hajo Hermann had already survived several brushes with death. This mission came the closest to costing him his life.

'We were more or less prepared for the next attack that Harris had announced. It seemed to cause a certain amount of panic. The people, women and children above all, were evacuated from Berlin, and I stood ready to join in the fight. I flew during the night of 23-24th August from Bonn-Hangelar to Berlin, and from a distance I could see that over Berlin an enormous firework display was under way. The flak shells and searchlights were shining and I noticed the first planes being shot down. Then I went into action.

'There was a bomber in front of me which I fired at but it escaped by spiralling away. I wanted to be more accurate with the next one and flew very close to it. But stupidly, I flew so close that I was lit up by the German searchlights below. So was he, and we fired at one another at almost point blank range. I could see the whites of his eyes, so to speak, and I suppose he could see mine.

'His plane started to burn and the crew had to bail out. He fired and hit my engine. Smoke began to pour from it and I had to bail out, too. I fell into a lake, wearing full war gear, in other words, an overall with the parachute but without anything such as a life jacket. I had to struggle to keep my head above water, and with great difficulty managed to swim ashore where I met one of the British crew. He was quite friendly. Later on, another member of the bomber crew was sent to a nearby hospital and I visited him there. What happened to me was a rather stupid affair, but at least Harris's bombers didn't return to Berlin for another two months, except in very small groups.'

In January 1944, the RAF staged a big attack on Hitler's headquarters. Once again, the Germans knew about it in advanced, having intercepted the British coded messages. When the raid took place, Hajo Hermann was in action again and once again brushed with death.

'The weather was quite bad. Nevertheless, I got my man in my sights and hit him. His plane started to burn, but just then, a large area of defensive lighting spread out over the clouds. I was more interested in seeing if the plane was going to crash and while that was going on, I became visible as a silhouette against the light beams.

'From behind me to the left, a Mosquito fired a salvo into my engine and everything was smashed up inside it. I got shrapnel in my leg and it was very unpleasant. At first I didn't notice that I was bleeding. I noticed it only when my leg became cold. I grasped it and saw what had happened. Well, I told myself, you'll have to do something to get down fast, and I flew towards the west because the weather looked as if it was better there.

'I managed to reach an area around Hagen in the Ruhrgebiet, near Dortmund, but I hardly knew what I was doing. I was in a very bad state, with bouts of blindness and thought I was going to fall unconscious. I said to myself, before I crash down below with the plane, I'll bail out and that's what

I did. I came through the clouds and snow storm and landed on the ground, but in really dreadful condition. I came down in a forest clearing, at about six o'clock in the morning, a door opened somewhere, some light shone and I called out, and some people quickly picked me up and drove me to a hospital. Fortunately, the hospital wasn't far away.'

The Mosquito that shot down Hajo Hermann belonged to the squadrons that were ranging virtually at will over German territory in the latter part of 1943. The Luftwaffe tried desperately to inflict losses and reduce the onslaught, but all that happened was that the Allied planes came over in increasing numbers. They were using new techniques - the 'pathfinder' system which located and marked targets by radar, and the strips of metalised paper known as 'window' which, when released in the air, jammed and confused Germany's own electronic defences.

The Luftwaffe could do little or nothing to prevent the systematic destruction of German towns, cities, factories and airfields. Hamburg was destroyed in July 1943, in a raid privately described by propaganda minister Josef Goebbels as 'a catastrophe the extent of which simply staggers the imagination'. The RAF bombed Wilhelmshaven and Peenemunde, where the V1 and V2, Hitler's 'vengeance' weapons, were being developed. The USAAF attacked the oil fields at Ploesti in Romania and the important ball-bearing factories at Schweinfurt.

Albert Speer, who became Hitler's Minister of Armaments in 1942 and took total charge of war production the following year, relocated and camouflaged factories and other important installations in an attempt to halt the severe disruption caused by the Allied bombing. The disruption nevertheless continued. Manufacturing capacity was decimated and the development of new weapons, such as the Me-262, was almost brought to a standstill.

Hermann Goering was still criticising the Luftwaffe, this time for not being able to stop the Allied bombers. Heinz Phillip, a fighter pilot, was one of the objects of his ire.

'When we were confronted with American air superiority, we practically became the hunted, we fighters, and because we hadn't shot down enough planes and the Americans arrived with the bombs and so on, Goering stood up and said, 'My fighters have become cowards'. In consequence, the entire officer rank removed their decorations and insignia and went around without their insignias of honour - Knights Crosses and so on, all gone.

'I couldn't stand Goering even before I was in the Luftwaffe. I regarded him as a vain, dressed-up fat man who performed like a theatre puppet. He wore fantasy uniforms - once he arrived in a snow-white uniform. He arrived in the morning, had a midday meal, inspected us, in the afternoon he did something

Take-off follows take-off, raid upon raid. The fighter pilot is ever ready to hurl himself upon the foe whenever encountered.

or other, he changed uniforms two or three times in that time. He was a vain caricature - the highest decorations, highest-ranking Marshal and God knows what else. I know of one incident when he was urgently needed but couldn't be found. Eventually, he was discovered at Karinhall, his palace. At Karinhall, there was a gigantic model railway in the cellar. Two or three men from the Luftwaffe had been assigned to him just to look after this railway, and there he was, playing with it.'

Early on in their campaign, RAF and USAAF bombers had been vulnerable due to the lack of fighter escorts that could accompany them all the way to Germany and back. This problem was solved in 1943 by the introduction of the P-51 Mustang fighters and, with these guards to protect them, the USAAF was able to resume the daylight raids that had been abandoned in 1943. This new Allied capability was typified by the 'Big Week' early in 1944 which saw continuous round the clock raids, in which RAF Bomber Command took over from the Americans at night. Between 20 and 26 February, the Allied air forces struck at the German aircraft and anti-aircraft factories and assembly plants in Leipzig, Regensburg, Augsburg, Fürth and Stuttgart. The Luftwaffe's attempts to halt the raids destroyed 244 heavy bombers and 33 fighters planes, but cost them 692 aircraft in the air and many more on the ground.

This was only part of the attrition suffered by the Luftwaffe and its pilots. By May 1944, the Germans had lost 2,442 fights in action and another 1,500 through accidents and although their air industry was not destroyed, the numbers of trained pilots lost were irreplaceable.

The Luftwaffe attempted to cut off the onslaught at source, by attacking airfields in England. Heinemann made two of these flights.

'We were sent on night fighter raids, with the bomber formations. We found the airfields in England were lit up brightly. I suppose they thought there would be no more Luftwaffe raids. We were supposed to give them some bother over there, but it proved much too dangerous. The raids were cancelled because too few of our planes returned.'

Meanwhile, the shortages occasioned by Allied attacks on Germany's oil-production facilities meant that training new pilots was curtailed for lack of fuel. Many Luftwaffe pilots going into battle for the first time at this late stage in the War were inadequately equipped to face the Allied challenge and all too often, they were soon shot down by the bombers or their fighter escorts.

Anton Heinemann, one of the Luftwaffe's night-fighter pilots, remembers the sheer impossibility of the task that faced them.

'Once the massing of the Allied planes began, you could theoretically shoot down perhaps one plane every half an hour, but the other ninety or hundred had already flown on, heading for their target. Our actual rate of 'kills' was no more

The squadron before starting for the north. The machines are drawn up as on parade and await commands.

than six bombers shot down in one night. We thought that was quite a lot. Once we shot down three, which was not so good.

'The problem was the opposing fire we encountered from the rear-gunners on the Allied planes. So, our aircraft were equipped with two guns facing vertically upwards. The rear gunners found it much more difficult to get at us as we flew under the bomber and fired up into its right side in order to make it burst into flames. That worked quite well. We were also given a follow-up round which was belted onto the gun so that we could destroy a bomber's fuel tanks. We used to pierce the tank, use an explosive shell which increased the size of the hole we'd made and another, incendiary, shell to start a fire.

'We used to fly mostly in a right-hand curve. The thinking behind this was that in our own aircraft, the pilot sat on the left and we assumed that it was the same in the enemy plane. When a plane caught fire, the Allied pilot wasn't going to turn onto the side that was burning. So, mainly they flew away to the left, in order to keep the fire above and not below, and I think that gave the crew a chance to bail out.

'The way we'd fired at the Allied planes was something of a secret weapon. I heard it reported that they were shot down by flak because they didn't know how we'd shot them down. I always hoped that the crew survived, but for us it was important that the plane and its bombs didn't get to its target.'

Heinemann himself had the experience of being shot down and bailing out to safety.

'In December 1943, my plane, a Junkers-88, was hit during one of the daylight missions we had to fly. We were going after a formation of American Boeings and were somewhere between Heligoland and Schleswig Holstein. There were about fifty American aircraft and they had such firepower at the rear that one of our engines was soon on fire, and we had to bail out

'It isn't difficult to make the decision to bail out when your engine is burning. All you know is the urge to escape. The Ju-88 had a hatch in the bottom, but when it was thrown open and produces such enormous suction, that if you just held out your boot then, Pphhtt! you were gone. We had been trained to count to about thirty before pulling the cord and then the parachute would open. On this occasion, I don't know why, I wasn't able to count to thirty. I got to about ten or twelve and then I pulled the cord. A rush of air got hold of me and I was pulled out of my felt boots. I remember seeing them get smaller and small down below because they were flying faster than I was with my parachute and disappear into the clouds.

'Then came the interesting question, Was I going to fall into the North Sea or land on the coast? Luckily there was quite a strong west wind and I landed in the area of Itzehoe, northwest of Hamburg, in an empty field. A man came rushing up. He was wearing a yellow badge which meant he was a Polish labourer and he said: 'Anglees, Anglees?' He thought an Allied invasion had begun and that he would soon be free. He was very disappointed.'

By the time Heinemann's Ju-88 was shot down, the American Eighth Air Force had opened up a new avenue of attack on Germany. Its P-51 Mustangs were let loose to search out the Luftwaffe fighters, embarking on a run of some 200,000 sorties during which they shot down 4,950 German aircraft and destroyed another 4,131 on the ground.

The Luftwaffe reeled before this onslaught. So many Luftwaffe aircraft were lost to this new strategy that Adolf Galland commented:

'The day the Allies took the fighters off close escort duties and allowed them to roam free to engage the Luftwaffe fighters in the air and on the ground was the day we lost the air war.'

The Luftwaffe was in no shape to challenge the greatest of all onslaughts during the Second World War: the D-Day invasion of Normandy on 6th June 1944, when the greatest amphibious force ever known to warfare assaulted Hitler's Fortress Europe. The air arm of the invasion carried out no less than 11,000 sorties and enjoyed complete superiority in the air from day one. Alfred Wagner was on his first combat mission when this mightiest of air umbrellas imposed its presence over northern France.

'When we heard that Allied paratroops and glider-bourne forces were in Caen, just before the main Normandy landings, we were stationed a long way away, at Biarritz, near Bayonne on the Bay of Biscay close to the Spanish frontier. We were awakened early in the morning and heard the news and were told we were going to be transferred north straight away.

'We were taken there on lorries, because we didn't have enough planes to fly there. On the way, we were attacked continuously by English fighter planes but managed to reach our destination while it was still dark. That was when I saw real, live war for the very first time. The fireworks, they were impressive and frightening at the same time. We were all very young, and we couldn't really comprehend it.

'We were quartered in a chateau, quite a comfortable place. There was a landing strip nearby and it was from there that we flew our missions. We flew in four planes in the direction of the front line. The flak came up at us, and you heard the detonation right next to your plane, and saw mushrooms when the shots exploded, directly beside you. It was a very unpleasant feeling. I don't know if it was enemy flak or 'friendly fire', but thank God, I wasn't hit.

'Then suddenly the enemy planes were there. I saw a Spitfire flying directly in front of me, but I managed to get away. I got separated from the other three planes and landed back at our airstrip on my own. That was my first mission

A group of combatant planes of the Heinkel He-11 type.

The order to start. An aircraftman is assisting a pilot to buckle on his safety-belt. The engines will be roaring in a few seconds.

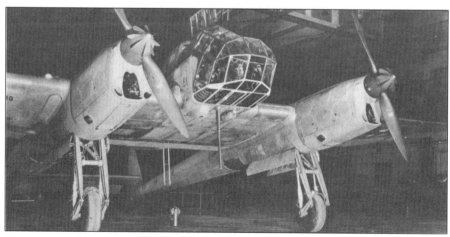

Front view of the Fw-189, showing the device retracting the undercarriage. The machine has just left the assembly bay and will soon, like so many others of its type, be leaving for the firing line to take up its responsible duties.

and it had been quite easy, I suppose except for the flak, of course.

'But later, things got really hot. We had to fly to wherever Allied fighters had been reported. We sighted them, and then it began, the swerving, the diving, like some terrible ballet we were performing. It was very nerve-wracking. You had to have eyes everywhere otherwise you could be 'jumped' by an enemy and that might be the end of you.

'Once, we had to attack a formation of Liberators directly head on. That was very dangerous because from head on, you had only about three second - two to fire your guns and then you had to make sure you got away. The Liberators or the Boeing B17s were so heavily armed that there was barely a blind angle to hide in. That's why we had to fire quickly when we attacked and get away fast.

'On one mission, an American Thunderbolt appeared in front of my snout, as they say. He tipped himself away to the right so that I could see the pilot quite clearly. He was black! A black American! We looked at one another, I pressed the trigger, there was an explosion and . . . he was gone. But I never forgot him. We had been eye to eye, opposite one another and that left a deep impression on me. It was frightening, and you said to yourself that the war was such madness; every war was. You shot down people you didn't know and would never know. It was terrible. '

Alfred Wagner discovered the hard way that the propaganda fed to the Luftwaffe pilots was totally untrue.

'At the beginning 1944, we'd been told that the Luftwaffe had a superiority in numbers of ten to one. The prospects looked good, especially after I'd shot down seven of those ten. But it was all a lie. When I was shot down myself, we were being attacked by three or four Allied planes at one time. So much for Luftwaffe superiority!

'On that occasion, my plane had problems on the ground. The engine was over-revving, and I noticed that the switch on the control equipment was on manual, when it should have been on automatic. The flight mechanic had been careless, I thought. I switched to automatic, and the number of revolutions dropped considerably. There was a huge wall of dust in front of me from the planes starting before me. I took off, but soon afterwards, reported myself out of service. I wanted to return to the airstrip, but then I looked up and saw a large formation of Thunderbolts above me.

'I didn't want to face them with a defective engine and looked about for somewhere to land unnoticed. But the Thunderbolts had seen me, and before I could do anything, a couple of them came down after me. I was hit from behind and saw flashes sparking from part of my wings. The wings were shredded. I felt a stab in my right foot. It must have been an explosive shell and my foot was shredded, too.

'My plane started to burn and I had to get out. I ejected the cockpit hatch, but couldn't push myself out properly because my right foot was useless. I managed to push myself out with my arms, and as I did so, my right arm struck the bodywork and the bone broke. Somehow or other, I don't know how, it must have been instinct, I pulled the ring of the parachute with my left hand, not something you normally did because you were taught to use your right hand. But if I'd tried to do that, I wouldn't have been alive now. I still can't understand how I managed to pull the parachute cord with my left hand. It was instinct, I suppose.

'The air battles in France took place quite close to the ground and my parachute had only just enough time to open. I managed to land all right, but quite far off in the distance I saw the mushroom cloud of smoke rising from where my plane had crashed.

'I was lying on the ground, fearing I would be shot while I was lying there, helpless. I shouted for help like a madman, and a French farmer came up over a nearby hill. He asked 'Allemande soldat?' - German soldier - and all I could say was 'Oui, toute, suite, hôpital!!' He said 'Doucement, doucement' - softly, softly, and went away.

'I went on screaming for help and another, older farmer came up and he asked: 'Allemande soldat?' I replied again: 'Yes, quickly, the hospital!'. This one ran away, too. After an age, or so it seemed, a car drove up and two military policeman and the second French farmer got out. The policeman was carrying a machine-gun. He was only two or three metres away when he started firing. I screamed, 'You stupid animal!' 'Oh,' he replied 'I thought you were an English Tommy.' They wrapped me in the parachute, carried me to the car and brought me to the hospital.'

Wagner's injuries were very serious. His right foot had gone and his right leg had to be amputated below the knee. He had lost the middle bone of his left foot and the fourth toe was missing, but he was alive, an outcome he ascribes to a certain spiritual resilience that surfaces at times of great danger.

'I think that at such moments, the human being is capable of superhuman achievement, superhuman strength'

Men at war have always had to live with the proximity of violent death or, perhaps even worse, crippling injury. Hajo Hermann had his own way of dealing with it.

'You may think the entire bird is going to fall to pieces, the plane's going to break up and that will be the end of you. But you just can't be continuously eaten up with such emotions. When something goes wrong, of course you get a big shock, but I used to say to my people: 'If there is a bang and bullets start

THE AIRCRAFT IN RETROSPECT: FW-190

In autumn 1937, the Reich Air Ministry commissioned designs for a new fighter to fight alongside the Messerschmitt Bf-109, which was then Germany's front line fighter. Although the Bf-109 was at that point an extremely competitive fighter there were concerns that future enemy designs might outclass the Me-109 and it was considered prudent to have new aircraft under development to meet future challenges.

The winning design was the excellent Fw-190 designed by Kurt Tank. It used the air-cooled, 14-cylinder BMW 139 radial engine, which produced improvements in air speed, manoeuvrability rate of climb and operating altitude. The Fw-190 was to prove one of the best all round fighter designs of the war and immediately outclassed the British Spitfires and Hurricanes. It continued in service throughout the war and lent itself to a continuous programme of research and development, which saw it in service as a fighter-bomber, high altitude fighter, night fighter and fast reconnaissance aircraft.

shooting through the cabin and the wind howls in, well, you can still think, you can still act. All right then, let's keep going. None of this trembling and dirtying your pants!'

During an attack on British ships at Le Havre at the time of the D-Day invasion in 1944, Hermann witnessed at first hand what could happen when nerves and anxiety took over.

'I'd borrowed this man from somewhere because my own navigator was ill. When we were about to make the approach run, he would keep saying: 'Are there barrage balloons? Is there going to be any flak? There are so many searchlights' and so on. Was I going to make a horizontal approach to the target? he wanted to know No, I told him, that won't be any good, we won't hit anything. I'm going to dive on the target.

'He said: 'Then I might as well bail out now!' 'Please do,' I told him. He stayed on board of course, but he made a grim face as if he wanted to murder me. Afterwards, when you pull the plane up and see those fat barrage balloons above you, then of course it's a bit frightening, but you have to say to yourself that the balloons aren't everywhere, you'll be able to get past them. This man moaned and groaned all the way back to base. We didn't fly into any wires, but frankly that was pure coincidence.'

Heinz Phillip knew what it was to be afraid, though he, too, developed his own method of keeping the fear at bay and even acquired a certain detachment about death in the air, whichever side in the War was doing the dying.

'You can't hear the flak exploding all round you, but you could see light. There was so much light when you're flying at around 3,000 metres You could read a newspaper by it and the flashes of explosions and tracer bullets. That's what it was like up there. You had a very empty feeling in your stomach and there were wet trousers, too, sometimes, There are people who said that they weren't afraid but I was afraid and most men were afraid too. 'Glorious, you just fly through it,' we used to be told. Not at all, that's just Latin, as we say in Germany, airmen's Latin.

'You just can't get away from the fact that you could be killed at any moment, so you try to distance yourself from death. When a comrade is killed, you try not to think about it too much. I was once playing a game called skat with three other Luftwaffe men. I had a marvellous hand, and so did one of the others. We kept on bidding and it was so exciting that other people in the room stood around watching us.

'Suddenly, there was an alarm. We threw down our cards, saying we would continue the game later. I was the first one back, so I sat there, cards in my hand, waiting for the other three to arrive. They never came. Then we were told that the pilot had crashed after take off and all three had been burned to death.

Maybe it didn't really register, but I said: 'Well, there must be someone around here who can finish this game.' There was, and so we finished the game.

'It worked both ways, for our opponents as well as for us. We never thought, at least I didn't and neither did our crew when we talked about it, we never thought that, if we shoot down an Allied plane, then we are going to kill ten people who are sitting inside. For us it was 'We are not killing the people, we are shooting down the plane.' That is an enormous difference. For us, the plane was the adversary.'

In the last week of July 1944, after seven hard-fought weeks, the Allies broke out of the Normandy beach head. By mid-August, the German forces were escaping eastwards, with the prospect that the Fatherland itself would soon be open to invasion. Meanwhile, on 15th August 1944, two months after D-Day, the Allies landed in the south of France. Heinz Phillip had his worst experience of the War as the Luftwaffe tried to prevent this second invasion.

'It was at Coulommières in the south of France. We'd been fighting all through the Allied disembarkation at night. We'd flown low level attacks on the beaches, and we returned to base and wanted to land. But when we were about to touch down, an English night fighter caught us at our most vulnerable moment. When the undercarriage and the ailerons are out, then the plane is as helpless as an old duck. The pilot of the nightfighter was a very good shot. He was directly behind us and when he fired, the radio operator was hit several times in the chest. Our aircraft was still able to fly, the engines were still running and our pilot retracted the ailerons and the undercarriage, accelerated and climbed back up into the air.

'But we were burning up, left and right, the wings - there are fuel tanks in the wings too and they were on fire. We wanted to bail out, I jumped, but my parachute got tangled in the plane. I was outside and the parachute was up there somewhere, so that I was just about able to look inside. The pilot, who was preparing to get out himself, saw that I was hanging there and he went back to the cockpit, set the plane straight and then he tried to kick me free with his foot. But that didn't quite work. He bailed out and the plane exploded. Only then was I free and although my parachute was rather shredded, I managed to land all right. But I landed very heavily. The time it took me to get from up there until I arrived down on the ground, it was only a few minutes, but it felt like an entire lifetime.'

In December 1944, the Germans made a desperate attempt to halt the Allied advance towards Germany by attacking the American 7th Army and other forces through the forested plateau of the Ardennes, on the border between Belgium and France. This brief, but doomed, campaign saw the last major offensive by the Luftwaffe, on 1st January 1945 when some eight hundred of

Flying and music have one overwhelming feeling in common; the sense of freedom, detachment, and triumph over the workaday world. All those listening there in small groups to the performance of a military band on a field airdrome may be animated by similar thoughts.

The flying crew of a bomber group seem to be enjoying themselves in the protection of their He-111 and are giving the musical interlude every attention.

their aircraft attacked airfields in France, Belgium and the Netherlands, destroying 156 Allied planes. It was an attempt to disrupt Allied air support, but it failed, with heavy losses. The Ardennes offensive cost the Germans a total of 1,600 planes and the Luftwaffe was finally broken.

The Me-262, the world's first turbojet fighter which first flew in combat in September 1944 came too late to save the Luftwaffe, or Germany. Its remarkable speed of 540 miles per hour, 140 miles faster than any conventional aircraft of its time, was wasted by Hitler when he ordered it to be used as an attack bomber rather than a fighter. Besides this, the Me-262 had cardinal faults, including engines with a service life of only twenty-five hours, and there were too few of them at this late stage in the War to make a difference to its outcome.

The moment the Luftwaffe and the Wehrmacht had struggled so hard to prevent came on 7th March 1945, when troops of the U.S. 9th Armoured Division broke into Germany across the Ludendorff Bridge over the Rhine at Remagen. German engineers were just preparing to blow it up when the Americans arrived. Heinz Phillip had volunteered for a mission to destroy the bridge. It was the only time his Ju-88 dropped bombs.

'Some volunteers were wanted and I took part, my pilot was always way out in front and I wasn't always filled with enthusiasm, but I had to go with him. A 5 cwt. bomb was attached below each of the wings left and right, and we were meant to drop them on the bridge at Remagen. Four or five planes in all went on this mission, which took place at night. But of course the Americans had gathered everything together at the Rhine crossing, everything they had, to defend themselves against air raids and it was quite some firework display that was staged there.

'For us it was not very good because we had drawn number three, in other words we were to be the third plane to attack. Each plane was given a time, and we knew, now the first one is attacking, and then there was a fireball and he no longer existed. Then, the second plane went in, that became a fireball too, except that it was a little lower down, and then it was our turn.

'You can image what our feelings were. It wasn't exactly lovely. But we made it. Admittedly we didn't hit the bridge, our bombs fell beside it, but we got out of it in one piece. But I'll never forget it, we had eighty-eight bullet holes in the plane by the time we got away.'

The world-tamed Heinkel bomber He-111, which has had a surpassing share in the success of the German operations in the present air war owing to its great fighting power and its speed.

Dr. Heinkel tries out an aerodynamic improvement with one of his closest co-workers on a model of the He-111.

On the traffic control tower of the international airport Berlin-Templehof, from which the air police have an uninterrupted view of the whole traffic of the airdrome.

BIBLIOGRAPHY

Ailsby, Christopher: 'Waffen SS' (Sidgwick and Jackson, 1999

Brown, Eric and Green, G. William (Editor): 'Wings of the Luftwaffe' (Airlife Books, 2000)

Bullock Alan: 'Hitler:A Study in Tyranny' (Penguin Books, 1990)

Burleigh, Michael: 'The Third Reich: A New History' (Macmillan, 2000)

Darman, Peter (editor) and Ripley, Tim: 'SS Steel Storm: Waffen-SS Panzer Battles on the Eastern Front 1943-1945' (Motorbook International, 2000)

Fugate, Bryan I: 'Operation Barbarossa' (Spa Books, 1989)

Hart, Stephen: 'The Wehrmacht' (Fitzroy Dearbourn, 2001)

Kaufmann, J.E. and H. W.: 'Hitler's Blitzkrieg Campaigns: The Invasion and Defense of Western Europe, 1939-1940' (Combined Books,1992)

Kershaw, Robert: 'War Without Garlands: Operation Barbarossa 1941-42' (Sarpendon Publishers, 2000)

Lewis, Brenda Ralph: 'Hitler Youth: The Hitlerjugend in War and Peace 1933-1945' (Spellmount Publishers, 2000)

Rauss, Erhard et al: 'Fighting in Hell' (Greenhill Books, London 1995)

Snyder, Louis: 'Encyclopedia of the Third Reich' (Robert Hale 1998)

MORE FROM THE SAME SERIES

Most books from the 'Luftwaffe in Combat 1939-1945' series are edited and endorsed by Emmy Award winning film maker and military historian Bob Carruthers, producer of Discovery Channel's Line of Fire and Weapons of War and BBC's Both Sides of the Line. Long experience and strong editorial control gives the military history enthusiast the ability to buy with confidence.

The series advisor is David McWhinnie, producer of the acclaimed Battlefield series for Discovery Channel. David and Bob have co-produced books and films with a wide variety of the UK's leading historians including Professor John Erickson and Dr David Chandler.

Where possible the books draw on rare primary sources to give the military enthusiast new insights into a fascinating subject.

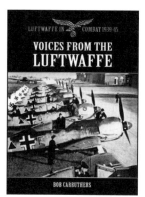

Voices from the Luftwaffe

Me.262 - Stormbird Ascending

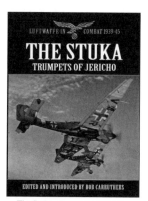

The Stuka - Trumpets of Jericho

Luftwaffe Combat Reports

Der Adler -
The English Language Editions

For more information visit www.pen-and-sword.co.uk